AF615951

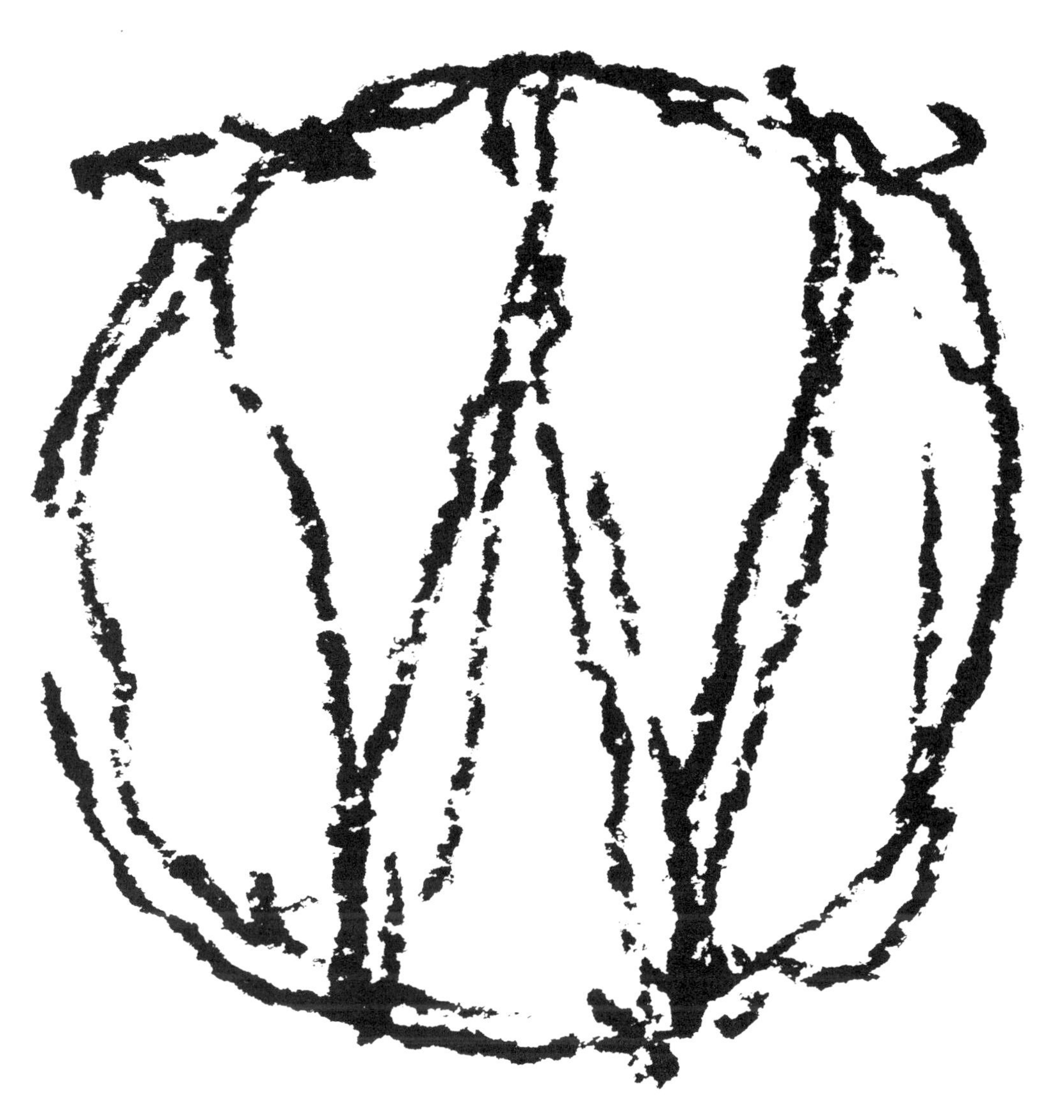

This exhibition was organized with the assistance of funds from the National Endowment for the Arts, the Minnesota State Arts Board and The Bush Foundation

Walker Art Center
9 December 1979–27 January 1980

Dallas Museum of Fine Arts
14 May–22 June 1980

The Denver Art Museum
19 July–31 August 1980

Des Moines Art Center
29 September–9 November 1980

San Francisco Museum of Modern Art
11 December 1980–25 January 1981

Library of Congress Catalogue Card No. 79-91533
ISBN 0-935640-00-2

Dimensions are in inches;
height precedes width precedes depth.
Dimensions described as a whole.

Front cover:
Mr. Unatural Eyes the Ape Run Ledge 1975
charcoal, colored pencil and wax on paper
36 x 28¾
Collection Robert and Nancy Mollers
Chicago

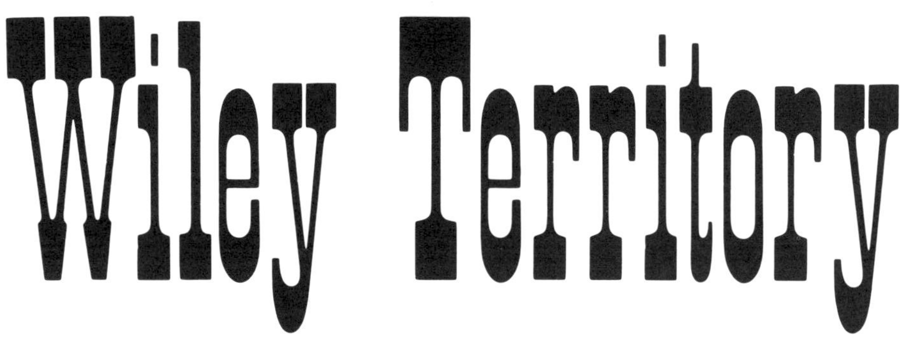

Wiley Territory

by Graham W. J. Beal
and John Perreault

Walker Art Center Minneapolis

Lenders to the Exhibition

Alice Adam
Stephen Alpert
Mr. and Mrs. Harry W. Anderson
Robert Arneson and Sandra Shannonhouse
Matthew and Wanda Ashe
The Baltimore Museum of Art
Mr. and Mrs. E. A. Bergman
Jacqueline and Myron Blank
Mrs. Alexander de Bretteville
Gilda and Henry Buchbinder
Mr. and Mrs. Gerald W. Bush
Cirrus Press, Ltd., Los Angeles
Mr. and Mrs. Byron Cohen
Crown Point Press, Oakland, California
Dallas Museum of Fine Arts
Mrs. Julius E. Davis
Delahunty Gallery, Dallas
The Denver Art Museum
Des Moines Art Center
Sarah Estribou
Roxanne Everett-Donald Lippincott Collection
Louis D. Fielder
Dr. and Mrs. Louis Fingerman
Fort Worth Art Museum
Allan Frumkin Gallery, New York
Frumkin & Struve Gallery, Chicago
Diana Fuller
John Garofalos and Mary Gremley
Goldyne Family Collection
Wally Goodman and Stan Picher
Graham Gund
Hansen Fuller Goldeen Gallery, San Francisco
Louis A. Hermes
Carl E. Horn
Elaine Horwitch
Indiana University Art Museum, Bloomington
Mr. and Mrs. William C. Janss
Landfall Press, Inc., Chicago
Modesto Lanzone's Restaurant, San Francisco
David Lawrence
Margo Leavin Gallery, Los Angeles
Los Angeles County Museum of Art
Mr. and Mrs. Lewis Manilow
Mr. and Mrs. Leonard S. Meranus
Byron R. Meyer
Robert and Nancy Mollers
Myra and Jim Morgan
Morgan Gallery, Kansas City, Kansas
Manuel Neri
Odyssia Gallery, New York
Ralph H. Perkins and Steven Smith
William H. Plummer
Judy and Joseph Raffael
Mr. and Mrs. C. David Robinson
CDR and Mrs. R. Rodriguez, USN (Ret.)
Mr. and Mrs. William Roth
Robert A. Rowan
San Francisco Art Commission, City and County of San Francisco and the San Francisco International Airport Commission
San Francisco Museum of Modern Art
Maxine and Jerry Silberman
William and Deborah Struve
Richard and Roselyne Swig
Walker Art Center
Whitney Museum of American Art, New York
Dorothy Wiley
William T. Wiley
Mr. and Mrs. William Wilson III
Yale University Art Gallery
Six Private Collectors

Acknowledgments

In the late 1960s, a number of young artists, dissatisfied with the limitations of pure abstraction, decided to pursue recognizable subject matter. To an older generation, for whom Abstract Expressionism was virtually a dogma, any concession to realism was revisionist. Whether it was indifference to criticism by their elders, youthful courage or sheer curiosity, for various reasons this younger group chose to describe the physical details of the world.

What now must be regarded as a realist revival took various forms, ranging from neo-academic approaches to latter-day Surrealism. For many artists, this new atmosphere encouraged a diaristic emphasis in which "realistic" subject matter was combined with personal symbols. Yet some artists, newly involved with subject matter, were reluctant to give up their abstract proclivities entirely, and their work constitutes a fluctuating amalgam of both polarities.

A leading figure among these was William Wiley, whose autobiographical images vary from realistic landscapes to large-scale, semi-abstract paintings in acrylic. He has continued to work in a variety of media and styles; a unifying characteristic of his work is a strong, incisive graphic quality. Another, and initially less obvious, unifying factor is a penchant for interposing himself in his works. Sometimes he appears, in surrogate form, as the tatterdemalion character, Mr. Unatural, with flying hair and flapping kimono, sometimes as the elusive being who leaves graffiti-like inscriptions embedded in paintings and sculptures.

Working with a prominent living artist, a stimulating process, is fraught with hidden dangers. William Wiley, however, has been the epitome of good will, submitting to interminable interviews and patiently answering endless questions about the diverse elements that comprise his work.

In organizing the exhibition, particularly in securing loans and photographing works for the catalogue, the Art Center staff relied heavily on the Hansen Fuller Goldeen Gallery in San Francisco. The Allan Frumkin Gallery in New York and the Frumkin & Struve Gallery in Chicago gave similar crucial support, and valuable assistance came from Wanda Hansen of San Francisco and the Odyssia Gallery of New York. The Morgan Gallery, Kansas City, Kansas, helped us secure several Midwest loans. We are very grateful to those individuals and museums who lent their work for the exhibition and tour. In doing so, they have expressed the spirit of the true collector. New York art critic, John Perreault, wrote a lively introductory essay for the catalogue which captures the spirit of Wiley's work.

Graham Beal, Chief Curator at Walker Art Center, organized the exhibition. He had invaluable opportunity to acquaint himself with the whole range of William Wiley's production and his lengthy interviews with the artist provided important clues to arcane themes that appear in the paintings and constructions. His enthusiasm for Wiley's work is evident in the scope of the exhibition and the critical essay he wrote for this catalogue.

Martin Friedman, Director
Walker Art Center

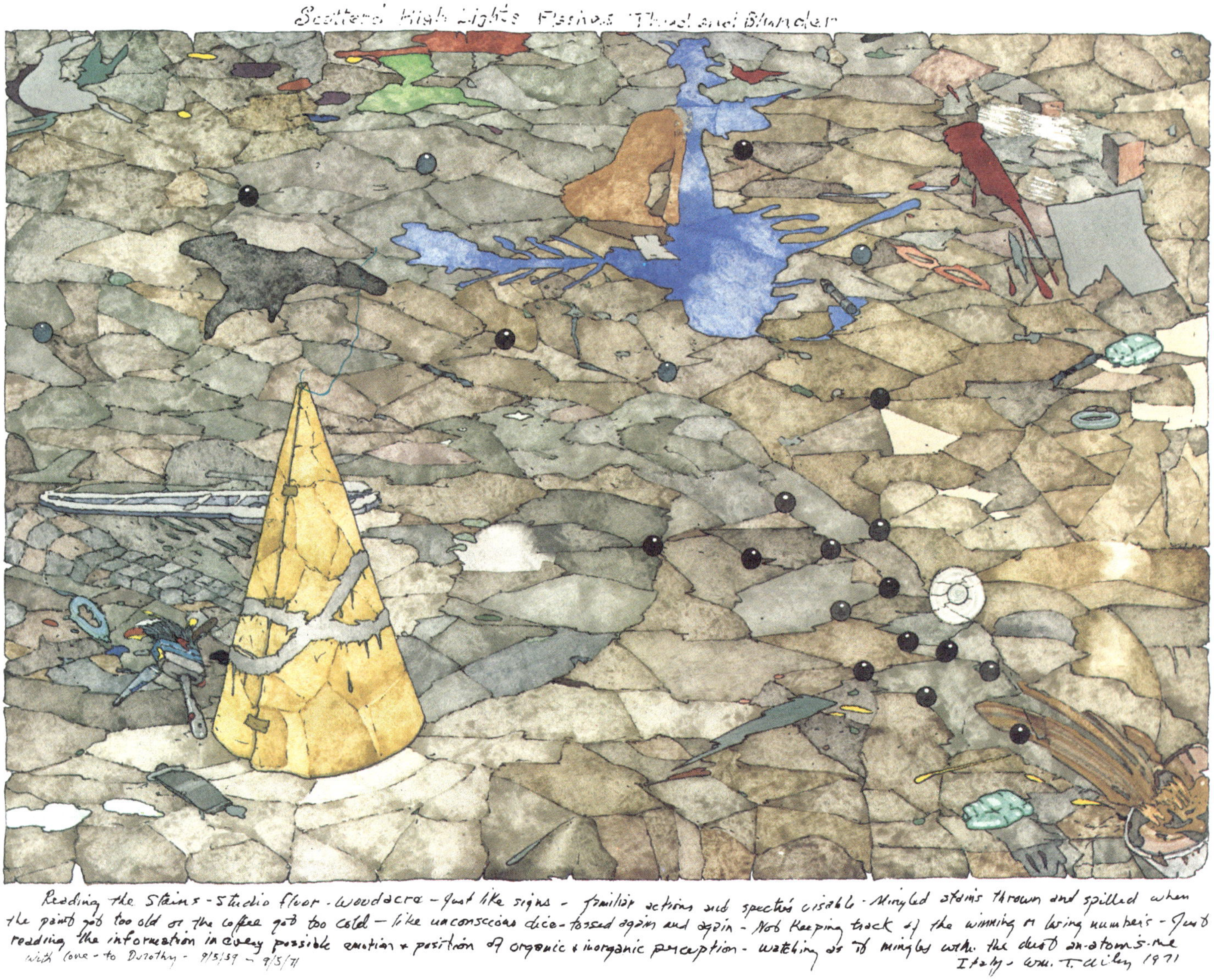

Reading the Stains 1971
watercolor and ink on paper
22 x 30
Collection Dorothy Wiley
Forest Knolls, California

Wiley Territory

John Perreault

What kind of art does William T. Wiley do? You have to see it to believe it. All other answers seem reductive or irrelevant. Recently I asked him how he answered a question like that and he replied with a fictionalized dialogue:

"So you're an artist?"
"Sure."
"Well, what kind of art do you do?"
"I do a lot of different things."
"Paintings?"
"Yes."
"Watercolors?"
"Yes."
"Representational?"
"I guess so."
"Landscapes?"
"Sure."
"Abstract?"
"In a way."
"Sculpture?"
"Yeah—and some writing too."[1]

The William T. Wiley territory covers a lot of territory. Obviously he does not believe an artist must stick to one medium or one genre. Yet, the results—watercolors, drawings, prints, paintings, sculptures and, recently, even murals (for the town of Hayward's Centennial Hall)—all come out uniquely his own.[2] The talent is there. Every mark, every image, every word seems to turn out just right, which is amazing considering that Wiley seems hell bent on exploring the arbitrary and the personal.

Wiley's work *is* extremely personal, but it is rarely self-indulgent or solipsistic. His fantasy content is that of everyday life. His art is loose and wacky as opposed to normal art, that resists "reading," viewer identification, and relationships to autobiography. Normal art is art that follows somebody else's rules and is usually boring. It does not add much to pleasure, to understanding, or to art. Wiley's art does.

---

1. All quotes from the artist are from an interview with the author in August 1979.

2. The murals, commissioned by the city of Hayward, proved controversial but have now been accepted. See "Wiley and Hayward Ponder Murals," *Allan Frumkin Gallery Newsletter*, Number 8, Spring 1979. Three 8 x 15-foot panels "describe" the possible uses of the Hayward Centennial Hall, the "history" of Hayward and its location within the Bay Area.

Wiley will not be pinned down to one art medium. He covers the field. This is not as unusual as one might think. What is unusual is that Wiley has accomplished something in every one of his endeavors; his art is curiously all of one piece. A particular mark of his genius—"genius" is an old fashioned word, but in this case I feel justified in using it—is that, for all the broad range of art activities he has investigated (played with?), one never gets the sense that he is spreading himself thin. Breadth and depth are constant. His work may be wry and ironically "folksy," but it is also poignant. There is beauty too: wrinkled, quirky, and with a touch of the oceanic in the larger works. His art seems to have conquered despair, in a tender rather than in a flashy way.

The breadth of Wiley's art activities may confuse some of his critics. But, to me, at a time when so many artists, because of narrow sensibilities (we cannot punish them for that), or because of commercial demands (which should only earn our disdain) have reduced their output to single-image wares, Wiley's adventurousness is exemplary. How did he achieve this impressive degree of freedom? The answer is complex.

Wiley himself admits that it took him awhile to get over the training he received at the San Francisco Art Institute and to regain the kind of freedom he had expected from art when in high school in Washington. Jim McGrath, his teacher, had allowed him and the other students (among them Wiley's life-long friends the artists Robert Hudson and William Allan) to touch all bases and all media in order to express themselves. ("Up until then I thought I'd get a ranch and some horses and draw cartoons like Red Ryder, continue that tradition.")

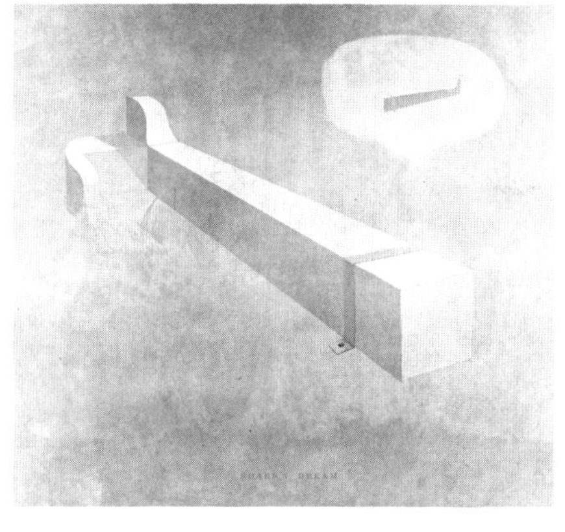

Shark's Dream 1967
William T. Wiley
oil on canvas
72 x 84
Collection Whitney Museum of American Art
New York
Neysa McMein Purchase Award

At the San Francisco Art Institute, where Wiley earned his B.F.A. and M.F.A., they taught strictly separated courses. "Painting and sculpture. But don't do both! The Clyfford Still kind of thing." In 1960, before he received his M.F.A., he had a one-man exhibition at the San Francisco Museum of Modern Art. By chance, I happened to see that show and I remember being impressed by Wiley's prodigious talent even then, when he was working in a late abstract expressionist style.[3]

In 1967 in New York, when I saw his *Shark's Dream* in the Whitney *Annual*—a painting of a bolted down, geometrical shark dreaming of itself in reverse—it was difficult to associate the work with the paintings I had seen seven years before in San Francisco. Was it the same artist? Indeed it was, but he had undergone a transformation. His new work was strange and, as I was not alone in pointing out, "metaphysical," perhaps related to de Chirico's pre-Surrealist visions.[4] As more and more of his work was shown, the change was even more pronounced. His exhibition at the Frumkin Gallery in New York that year, including watercolors and constructions as well as paintings, was astonishing.

---

3. Dore Ashton
"Abstract Expressionism Isn't Dead"
Studio International, September 1962,
pp 104-105.

4. Dore Ashton
"Quid est? '... for an Answer, only Enigma'"
Arts, March 1968, pp 46-48.

The Great Metaphysician 1917
Giorgio de Chirico
oil on canvas
41⅛ x 27½
Collection The Museum of Modern Art, New York
The Philip L. Goodwin Collection

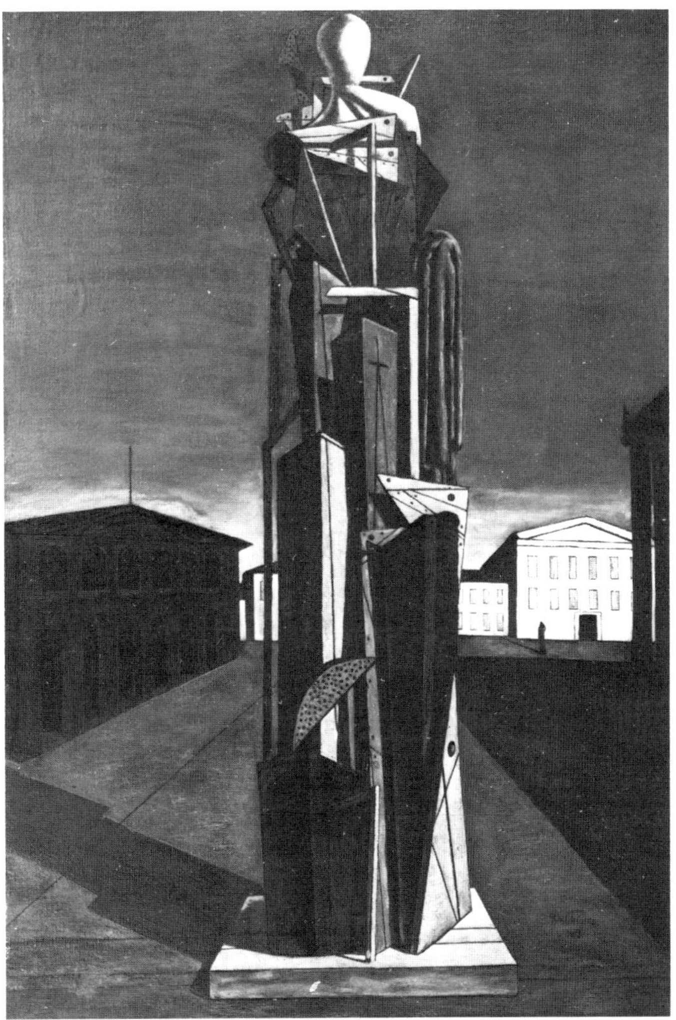

After his San Francisco Museum show, Wiley admits his dissatisfaction with his work and that he was plodding along. Teaching came to the rescue: "Getting out of the San Francisco Institute, I was frustrated with my painting. So, initially, teaching was fantastic... being able to take the energy somewhere. I didn't know if I could do it. But I said I'd try it for awhile. I needed a job. It turned out I really liked it."

Wiley taught at the then new Department of Art at the University of California, Davis campus. No doubt his presence helped make it the important art school it rapidly became. But in an unusual turn of events it was the students who influenced him. Wiley, who is most generous to other artists, gives them a great deal of credit.

> Teaching was fantastic. I ran into some good students, people better than me: Bruce Nauman... and Steve Kaltenbach were students; David Gilhooley and Robert Arneson, that whole group of people. It just all bubbled. It was great, because I liked what everyone else was doing more than what I was doing myself.

Had they influenced him? "Oh, yeah. I connected right away with what Nauman was trying to do. Hard-edge and Minimal were just coming in and Bruce's work was related to that, but it was kind of a dumb version, a looser attitude. I think that's what my work sprung out of. Those ideas were bubbling in my head and he had figured out how to get it out there. There were certain appreciations and sensibilities we shared. And then there was all that anti-form work developing and I felt very touched and moved, just watching that happen."

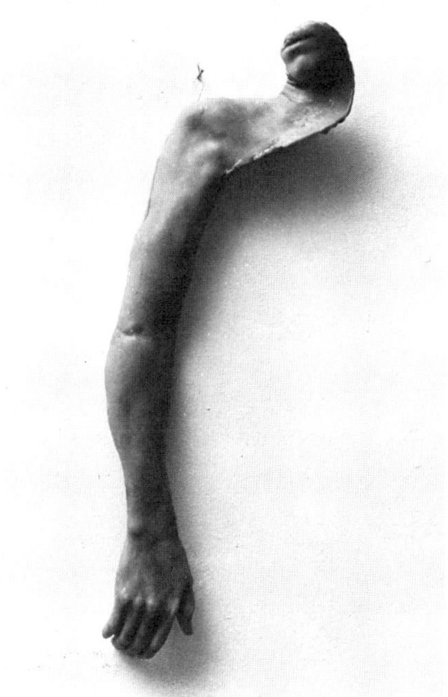

From Hand to Mouth 1967
Bruce Nauman
wax over cloth
30 x 10 x 4
Collection Joseph Helman
New York

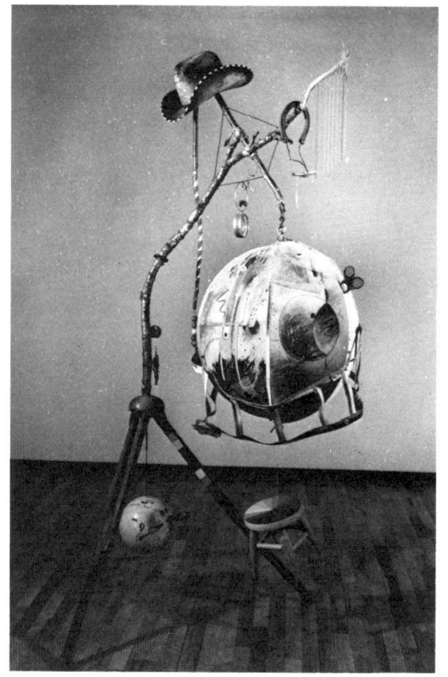

Cowboy Saddlelight 1974
Robert Hudson
mixed media sculpture
91 x 41 x 28
Courtesy Allan Frumkin Gallery
New York

Art influences among contemporaries are difficult to track. The art network is made up of smaller networks or clusters, the vectors or channels of which are often two-way. William Allan's and Robert Hudson's influences upon Wiley or his upon them, for instance, are impossible to untangle. These artists are all lifelong friends. A sense of the absurd, a celebration of the ordinary, and a love of materials seem to be a common ground. Allan's allegorical paintings—an open penknife and a fish floating over a mountain landscape is one set of images that comes to mind—and his straightforward trout fishing watercolors, clearly indicate a sensibility that overlaps with Wiley's. Hudson's work exhibits a harder, brighter palette than Wiley's, but shares—particularly in terms of the constructions—a devil-may-care exploitation of oddments and artifacts held together in zany ways.[5]

Wiley's sensibility also overlaps that of the innovative West Coast ceramic artists, who, beginning in the late 60s, reclaimed clay for serious sculpture, letting loose a barrage of witty clayworks, ranging from the willfully gross to the ironic and the playful. Robert Arneson, one of the most widely acclaimed of these artists, has even produced a magnificent bust of Wiley as the artist's alter ego, Mr. Unatural.[6]

---

5. Peter Schjeldahl
Robert Hudson
Moore College of Art, Philadelphia
1977 (catalogue).

6. Beth Coffelt
Robert Arneson
Moore College of Art, Philadelphia
1979 (catalogue).

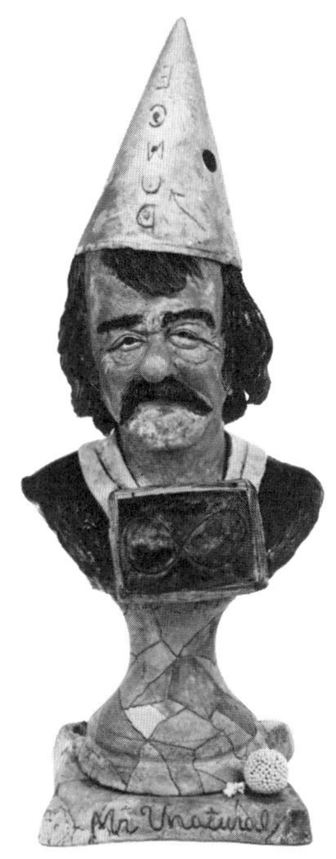

Mr. Unatural 1978
Robert Arneson
glazed ceramic
53½ x 22 x 22
Courtesy Allan Frumkin Gallery
New York

Wiley also mentions Joan Brown and other Bay Area "Funk" artists as influences, remembering that he was particularly impressed with Manuel Neri's plaster works that were destroyed after they were exhibited. But, as Wiley generously admits, it was his student Bruce Nauman who had the most liberating effect on him. Nauman, now an artist with an international reputation, is considered an important contributor to the so-called anti-form or process mode of art-making that emphasized ordinary, non-traditional materials and relaxed, randomized or conceptualized ways of producing art work: a floor "sculpture" made of studio sweepings, body casts, etc.[7]

I wondered what other artists Wiley saw as an influence.

Duchamp. A lot of people from the Surrealist-Dada territory. I have some affinity for what was going on. And I like H. C. Westermann: the humor, the solidity, the simplicity, the tangible materials, the double-edged landing on all those territories.

But Wiley has not given much thought to whether or not he is continuing the Dada-Surrealist tradition: "Neo-Dada and Dude Ranch Dada don't concern me very much. When I was back East I realized a kind of primal motivation and connection with art."

Marcel Duchamp is often considered the most Dada of the Dada artists. His readymades (a bicycle wheel mounted on a kitchen stool, a bottle rack, a snow shovel titled *In Advance of the Broken Arm*—selected or "found" rather than made) were proposed as art works around 1913. They still have the power to shock and to cause doubt about their own status as art—although they have been institutionalized as such—and to cause doubt about the nature of art in general. Duchamp's influence was miraculously reactivated in the 60s, for his early work seemed to foreshadow the common imagery of Pop art and other concerns: the use of chance, irony, non-art materials, process and intellectual content. On the surface one might see Wiley (the down home American "cowboy") and Duchamp (the Parisian dandy) as opposites, but Duchamp's anti-pomposity has obviously provided an inspiration and an example for Wiley in his own pursuits.

H. C. Westermann is another Wiley hero.[8] Westermann is an "original" and an artist's artist and, like Wiley, deals on some level with male fantasies. In Westermann's case, the high seas get their due. Mystery houses, sinking ships and ice cream cones of tar are lovingly crafted into special surrealistic Americana. Wiley's work too exhibits both craftsmanship and an aura of dreams.

---

7. Robert Pincus-Witten
"Bruce Nauman: Another Kind of Reasoning"
Postminimalism (London: Out of London Press, 1977) pp 70-78.

8. Barbara Haskell
H. C. Westermann
Whitney Museum of American Art
New York, 1978 (catalogue).

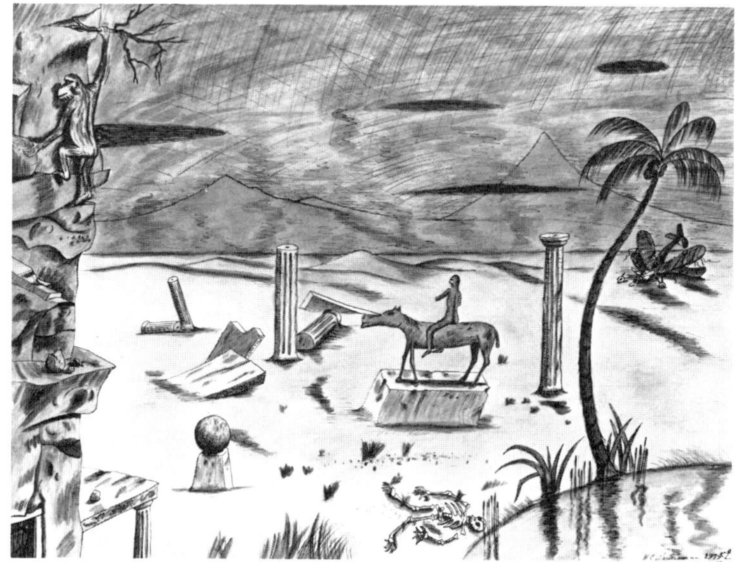

The Lost Mines of King Solomon 1979
H. C. Westermann
watercolor
22¼ x 31
Courtesy Xavier Fourcade, Inc.

After a trip to Europe, during 1967 and 1968 Wiley spent nine months on the East Coast. He had a temporary teaching job at the School of Visual Arts in New York and was living with his family in New Jersey. I visited him and talked with him to prepare for an article I was writing about his work for *Art News*.[9] I was unaware, however, that he had passed through a kind of dark night of the soul and had so recently achieved a clear breakthrough in his work and in his thinking about art:

Why do you want to do it? A whole lot of material and information had sifted between me and making art. That winter in New Jersey I sort of hacked back to the source. Like, wow, I've been putting in all that energy worrying about that stuff and that's okay. But it's a little bit beside the point. There's a lot more basic connection between me and what I do and why I do it. The simplest analysis is that art is something I love doing. Having made that peace, that was pretty connecting... All that spiritual stuff that was happening in the 60s was perfect. It was surrender, you know? I said to myself, "I can't do it any more, keep everything separate. I'll just fall over dead.

That was the longest period I spent without working. Five, six months. That was the first time I thought maybe I'm not supposed to be an artist. It was sure bleak at that point. I think it's in there, but it won't come out. Maybe I've got to give up, just stop. It's okay. Now what's going to happen? Well, I still have my teaching job. I'll go back and hang on until they sling me out.

I took off all the critic and judge business. I'd go to New York and look at a lot of art. If it made sense to me, okay. If not, okay. Everybody's doing the best they can. I had a real amateur status attitude about it. It was really an amoral thrill. At that point, Duchamp started to make sense and a whole lot of things started falling into place. I just felt so happy getting my work together. If somebody liked it that was terrific. It was after the fact. It was the first time that either positive or negative criticism was useful to me. I didn't have anything to defend.

Where Does Wiley fit? He is certainly not a minimalist. His work is too "impure." Although there are sometimes conceptual overtones in his work and a definite narrative content, he is not a conceptualist; his work is too much concerned with touch and physicality. His work is too visual to be Idea art. Although his work has representational elements, he is certainly not a realist: fantasy and myth get in the way. He is inordinately difficult to classify, which is one of his strengths.

---

9. John Perreault
"Metaphysical Funk Monk"
Art News, May 1968, pp 52-53+.

But perhaps because he is one of the few non-New York based artists to gain national prominence, he is in a sense a regionalist. He certainly offers a ray of hope to all those artists and would-be artists who for some strange reason do not want to elbow their way through the art hordes in New York's Soho district, who like where they are living and are nourished by particular places, cities, landscapes. He is one of the best West Coast artists to emerge during the past dozen years; some might say the only one of national significance. If there is anything particularly California or Bay Area about his work, I am yet to be convinced. Wiley's West is everybody's—a national fantasy derived from cowboy movies and comic books. He lives in Marin County, California, not in Tucson or Tombstone. Garages and backyards are as much a part of his fictionalized landscape as the California Gold Rush or the Pacific Frontier.

Another classification that comes up is Funk. I have used that classification myself. The 1967 *Funk* show at the University of California at Berkeley not only created a new art term, but also helped put a number of Bay Area artists on the art map.[10] Wiley was in that show. Wiley himself feels that whatever Funk was—in part it was an anything goes reaction to the lack of a local support system—it was mostly over with by the time of the show. Funk art was never a real art movement. Using the term now suggests a time warp. "Funky" images and materials—non-art resources for art—were given official approval, and that created some degree of energy, but Funk art now is itself in a funk. With all the various artists now off in their own "territories" (as Wiley might put it), Funk art is an empty category.

My conclusion is that Wiley is impossible to classify. One might ask, but is he mainstream? He's better than that. He is one of the most important artists to challenge the very notion of "Mainstream" art. His work has already added a great deal to art: his inventiveness, his laid-back wit, his humanistic humor. He has helped open up art to kinds of personal expression that the modernist academy had forbidden. His daring art has been of enormous influence.

Is he an innocent? I think not. His obvious "fine art" skills remove him from the realm of the naive. And although it may be difficult to grasp his apparently total disregard for his place in art history—his work is more important than its ranking in some hierarchy—if he is an innocent at all, he is such by virtue of a high degree of art sophistication.

It is becoming more and more apparent that he is a major artist. His seriousness is in no way undercut by his quirky, sometimes tongue-in-cheek, sometimes paradoxical vision. In fact, this vision is at the center of his art. Those smiles his works so often cause are smiles of recognition, smiles of glee. The foibles and the homey triumphs that he chronicles—in a grand flood of images, objects, textures, markings and words—signify personal and artistic release.

10. Peter Selz
Funk
University of California, Berkeley, 1967
(catalogue).

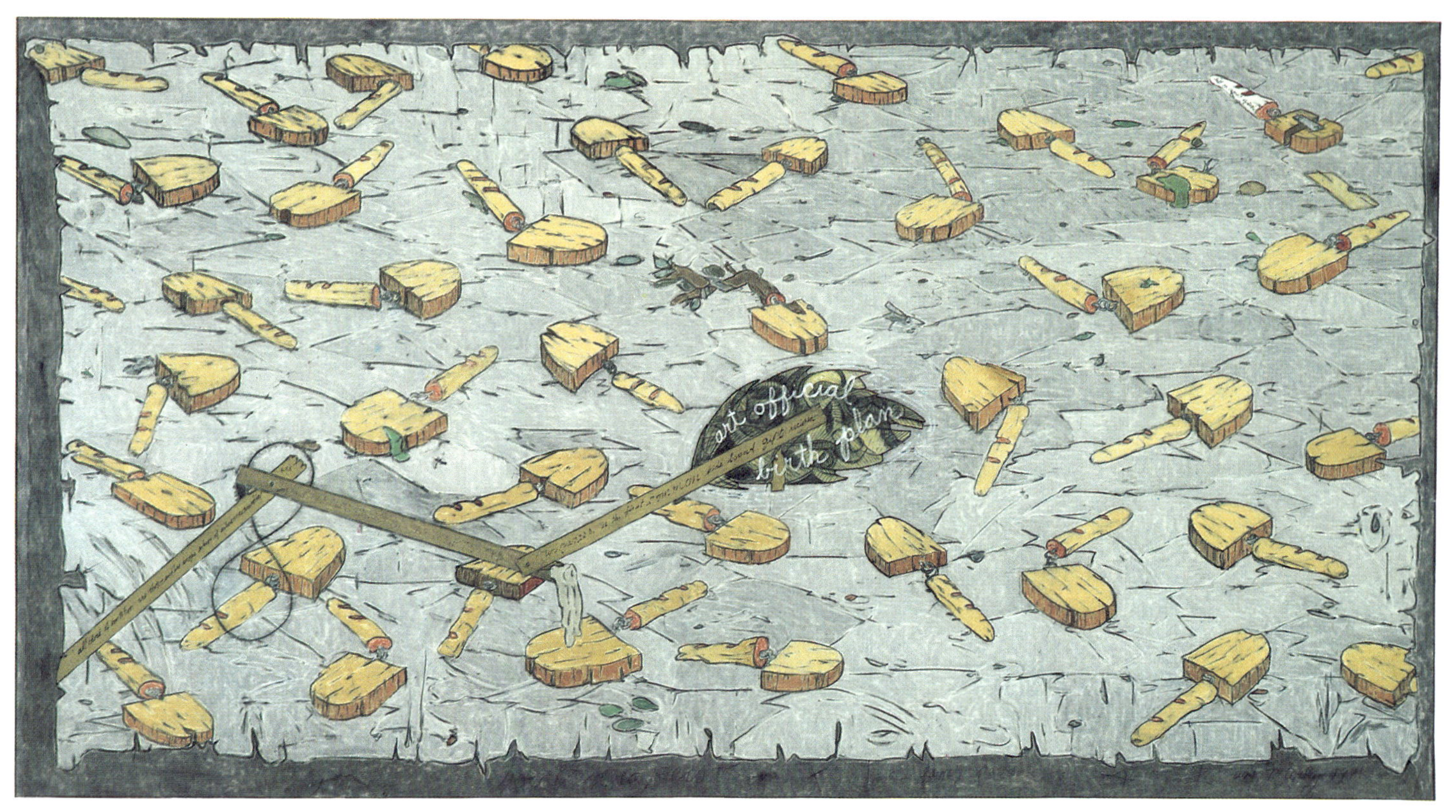

Art Official Birth Plan 1971
acrylic and charcoal on canvas
84 x 153
Collection Mr. and Mrs. Harry W. Anderson
Atherton, California

The Beginner's Mind

Graham W. J. Beal

In the beginner's mind there are many possibilities, but in the expert's there are few.

Shunryu Suzuki, *Zen Mind, Beginner's Mind*

William Wiley lives in Marin County, California, land of hot tubs, good wine and easy times, where, as the saying goes, "I'm O.K., you're O.K.," and all is well when "you find your own space." Such attitudes—easily pilloried as unabashed egoism, devoid of philosophical vigor—represent only the superficial layer of far-reaching attitudes that have shaped society and influenced artistic activity on the West Coast.

In a cultural phenomenon that confounds Rudyard Kipling's expressed belief that "East is East, West is West and never the twain shall meet," disparate forces such as the tough individualism that conquered the wild West and the beatific spirit of Zen Buddhism have come together. Trying to untangle the strands is an interesting, often frustrating, exercise, and nowhere are they more intertwined than in the work of William T. Wiley.

His art *looks* western enough, both in its relation to the Dada-Surrealist tradition (Marcel Duchamp, Giorgio de Chirico and René Magritte, in particular) and in the world he invariably depicts, that of northern California. But pervading the occidental appearance of Wiley's art is the elusive, oriental presence of Zen Buddhism.

That Wiley has been able to combine the jesting nihilism of Duchamp and the disturbing psychology of Surrealism with the optimistic pantheism of Zen is one of his most impressive achievements. In doing so, he created a potent, unmistakable style that, though seized upon by a generation of younger Bay Area artists, nevertheless remains essentially inimitable.

In the late 60s, when minimalism and hard-edge abstraction dominated the art scene in New York and Los Angeles, Wiley adopted a perversely old-fashioned style. Small images, composed of many little bits and pieces fitted together like a jigsaw puzzle, were quaintly rendered in watercolor—a medium redolent of 19th-century associations. At a time when a "cool," impersonal approach to subject matter was the rule, Wiley became aggressively autobiographical, drawing upon his own erratic thought processes and the circumstances of his day-to-day life.

The style for which Wiley is best known seemed to arrive fully formed in 1967, and in one sense this is the case. In that year, Wiley underwent the personal revelation outlined in John Perreault's essay: that he could sculpt or paint in any way he wanted, without concern for critical opinion. His sense of relief was so great that Wiley has referred to this period as one of "Enlightenment." The change in his art, both in form and philosophy, was dramatic.

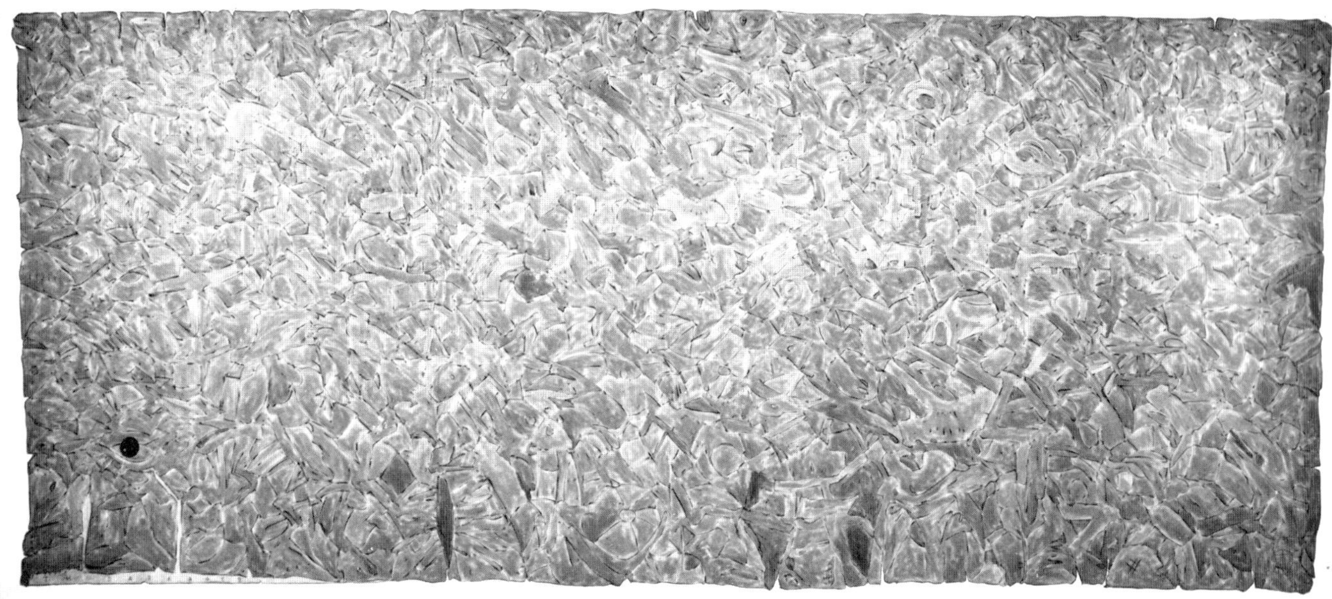

Thudarkages 1972
acrylic on canvas
84 x 192
Collection Des Moines Art Center
Coffin Fine Arts Trust Fund, 1973

While on sabbatical in England, Wiley had acquired a small, easily portable set of watercolors, and he turned to this medium when, after his six-month period of inactivity, he started to paint again. In a group of watercolors, epitomized by *Brush Exploding in Space*, 1967, Wiley arrived at a new way of working—one of several directions he has pursued ever since. Small in format, with clear, delicate colors, these images have an intimacy ideally suited to the quiet, quirky, autobiographical character soon to be predominant in his work. In a process that he still favors, Wiley first outlines an image in felt-tip pen. He then fills in the web of black lines with watercolor, blotting with paper towel as he moves from one small area to the next, to maintain an even texture. In the best of these watercolors—the glowing 1969 landscape, *Lame and Blind in Eden*, for example—the deep, illusionistic space of the landscape is countered by the bright colors and the network of black lines, and the impression produced is not unlike that of a stained glass window.

The quality of fragility that characterizes the new watercolors was carried over into other media—the larger acrylic paintings and constructions. The acrylics, unlike the intimate watercolors, lean towards the abstract, but the technique employed in large paintings such as *Thudarkages*, 1972, is dependent upon a method evolved in the watercolors: that of drawing small, interlocking components and then filling them in with paint.

The space in Wiley's large canvases, in contrast to that of the watercolors, is shallow. The almost totally flat, rocky terrain of *Art Official Birth Plan*, 1971, is repeated in intensely hued paintings of the same period. In a work such as *Village Green*, 1974, the painted field equivocates between shallow, cubistic depth and a personal system of cartography. A number of Wiley's watercolors draw their strength from the ambiguity of the depicted space, as in the soft-toned *Reading the Stains*, of 1971, in which Wiley's studio floor is transformed into an imaginary landscape. We are reminded of Leonardo da Vinci's words: "You should look at certain walls stained with damp, or stones of uneven color. If you have to invent some setting you will be able to see the likeness of divine landscapes... because from a confusion of shapes the spirit is quickened to new inventions."[1]

In his new sculpture, the industrially fabricated, geometric forms Wiley had preferred in sculpture before 1967 gave way to ramshackle constructions incorporating tree stumps, branches, bits of leather and bones, "found objects" such as toy cars, light bulbs and license plates. In the sprawling 1972 construction, *Modern Skullpture with Freaknest*, slender tree branches curve around a battered styrofoam ball held in tension by bits of string, as Wiley "draws in space," transposing the apparent fragility of his watercolors into literally fragile, three-dimensional form.

Crucial to Wiley's mature style is his use of written narrative. Ranging from philosophical musings to fragments of tales and short poems, Wiley's scribbled inscriptions have been interpreted variously as "jokes" made at the expense of the observer, or as an inability to be serious. Both readings are wrong; these tangential, written inclusions allow Wiley to express thoughts that cannot assume visual form but, occurring during the creation of a work, are relevant to its final image. The inscriptions introduce unexpected ideas and imbue mundane objects with disturbing qualities.

In *Twice Upon A Time*, an innocuous looking 1975 watercolor of a knife in a tree stump on the studio floor, the words underneath imply that the log is a metaphor for the human body. Phrases such as, "Who's the cutest organism in Dos Puentes?... a trunk full of impulses... like a large dissolving brain... a shape we call Mother's," can introduce disquieting, erotic overtones.

Wiley's writings are meditative. He never actually tells a story. Even *Suite of Daze*, 1975-77, a series of etchings in book form, emphasizes aphorism at the expense of description. Wiley's intuitive approach is reminiscent of that of the English romantic, William Blake, to whom writing and painting were inextricably related. On the subject of spiritual antecedents, the form of Wiley's watercolors owes something to Leonardo da Vinci's notebooks, the *look* of which, in terms of intimacy and immediacy, Wiley has always preferred to the Renaissance master's paintings. And Wiley's watercolors, while not lacking in spontaneity, have the jewel-like quality of medieval manuscripts. In his works, the carefully delineated image serves much the same purpose as an elaborately illuminated initial.

---

1. Leonardo da Vinci
Trattato della Pittura
Translated by Kenneth
Clark in *Leonardo da Vinci*
Harmondsworth, Middlesex, England:
Penguin Books Ltd., 1967, p 82.

Twice Upon a Time 1975
watercolor and ink on paper
30 x 22
Collection Dr. and Mrs. Louis Fingerman
Des Moines, Iowa

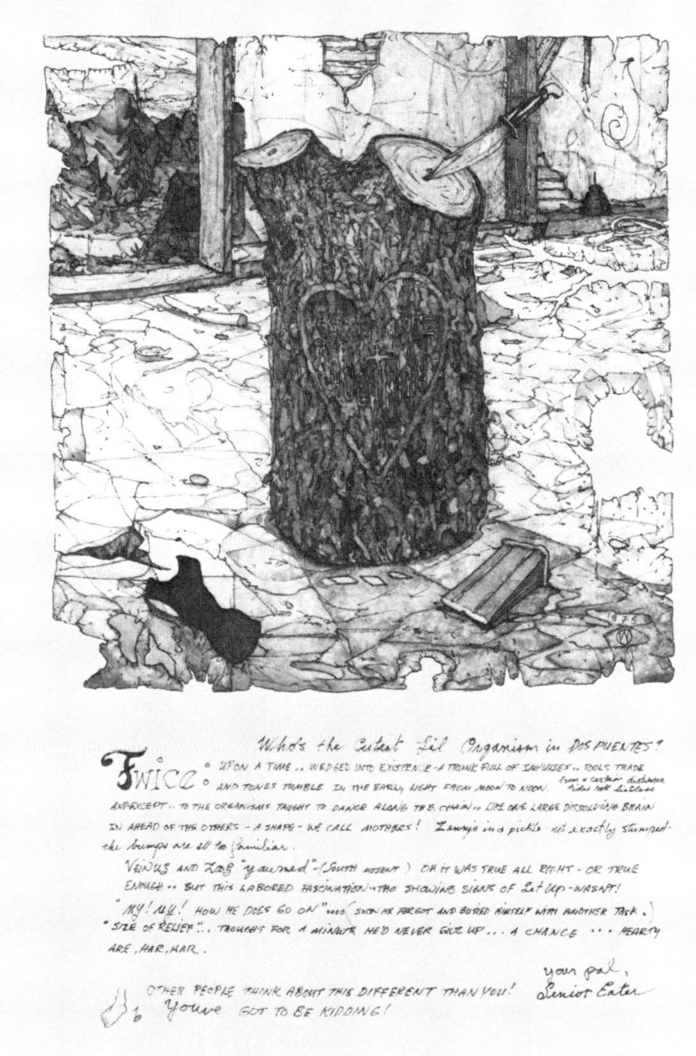

Wiley's use of the pun in his writings parallels the mutative process that informs his complex, quasi-secretive imagery. Punning titles, such as *Art Official Birth Plan* (try Artificial Birth Plan) and *Lord Half Mercy* (or Lord Have Mercy) encourage quite disparate interpretations of a single work of art. More common in Wiley's titles than the simple pun is a phrase—often extracted from colloquial speech—capable of different interpretations. In the titles, *Nothing Changes*, *The Glittering Remains*, *Certain Things No One Can Teach You* and *It Remains to be Seen*, meaning can shift, depending upon where emphasis is placed.

By 1971, Wiley's mature style was established. Three basic categories, based on technique, have been outlined above, but there is considerable overlap and frequently constructions are exhibited alongside paintings or watercolors in a single work. In the 1977 "magnum opus," *The Hound Harbor Series*, a large, boat-like construction is accompanied by two paintings, one large, one small, and a drawing.

Although the work embraces a wide range of materials and forms, his basic approach is that of drawing. Sure, meandering lines that define the patchwork areas of Wiley's watercolors and paintings, slyly lead us from one beguiling discovery to another. Our eye "bumps" against unexpected objects in much the same way as words and phrases leap out of the fragmentary, written narratives that invariably are found in Wiley's paintings.

To pursue this idea on a metaphorical level, Wiley's approach to sculpture is essentially "linear." His constructions are built up over a period of time by an additive process. Objects are incorporated or removed as, stimulated by the forms around him, Wiley moves from one idea to another.

Around 1975, a shift towards greater description and less abstraction occurred within Wiley's style, but more realistic modeling of form is counteracted by the way objects and people—indeed, whole scenes—are made to overlap with one another, producing startling juxtapositions of unrelated objects. In the large 1978 canvas *Traced Home*, skulls, guitars, coats and figures materialize from the dense, linear network. In acrylic paintings of this period, the allusive landscape forms have been replaced by specific, topographical features: the pools, rivulets and houses of *Painting for Rain*, 1976. Rather than attempt to separate elements exactly, Wiley says he decided to "let things drift back and forth... I was amazed to find that from different distances, realistic forms had the same function as the more abstract, organic ones and that other forms, not consciously drawn, would occur out of the overlapping."[2]

Two sub-categories can be identified in Wiley's works on paper since 1975: drawings and watercolor sketches. Both groups share some characteristics of the large canvases of the last five years. In the 1975 charcoal drawing, *Studease for Post O.O.W. II, Mr. Unatural Confrontself*, no less than three figures appear out of a welter of rapidly drawn lines. In the diminutive 1976 watercolor, *North of Martial*, vague landscape forms resolve from the dashed off, impressionistic brushstrokes.

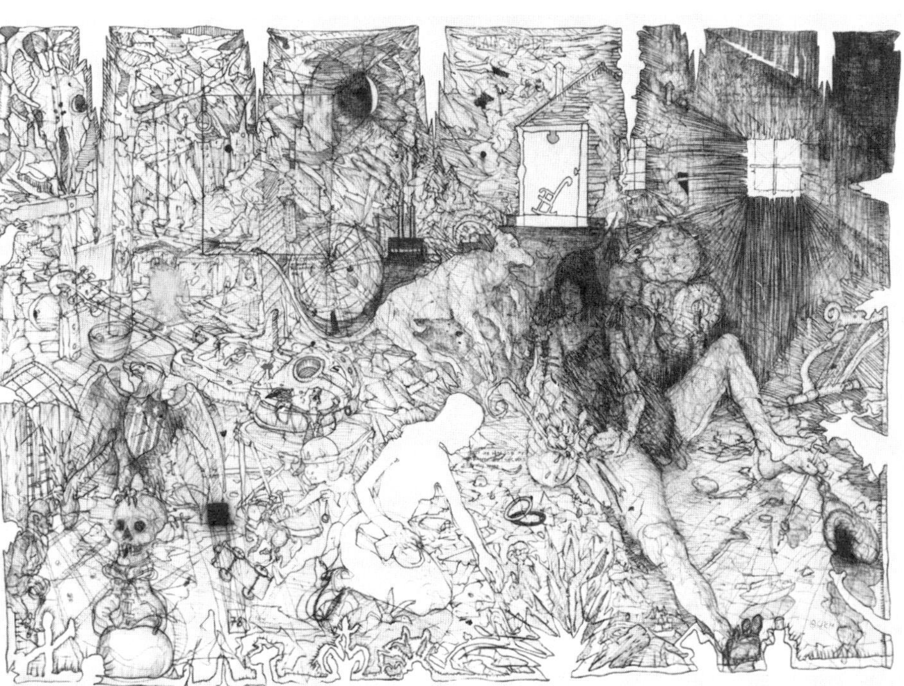

Traced Home 1978
acrylic and charcoal on canvas
84 x 114
Collection Mr. and Mrs. Byron Cohen
Shawnee Mission, Kansas

2. Unless otherwise indicated, all quotations from William Wiley are from a series of interviews conducted by Graham Beal in December of 1978 and June of 1979 at the artist's house in Forest Knolls, California.

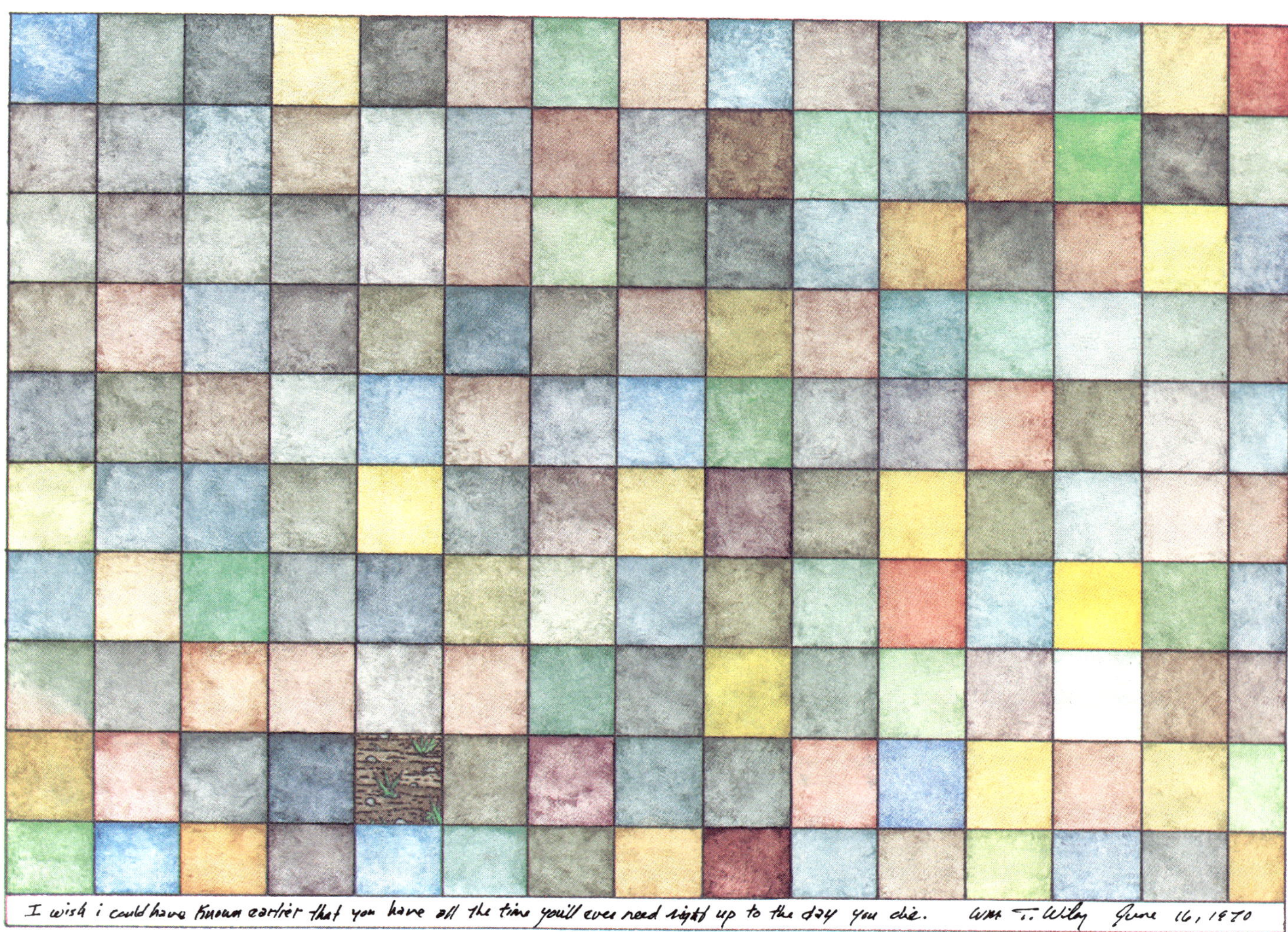

I Wish I Could Have Known Earlier That You Have All the Time You'll Need Right Up to the Day You Die 1970
watercolor and ink on paper
22 x 30
Private Collection

Before you have studied Zen, mountains are mountains and rivers are rivers; while you are studying it, mountains are no longer mountains and rivers no longer rivers. But once you have had Enlightenment, mountains are once again mountains and rivers are rivers.

Zen Saying, Anonymous

No understanding of Wiley is complete without some awareness of the effect of Zen Buddhism on his art and life. Though he has never studied Zen in a systematic way and most of his understanding comes from friends or from his own reading, he possesses that rare sense of inner balance and peace of mind frequently associated with Eastern sages. In a typically reticent fashion, he will comment, "I've absorbed enough to say that I don't know anything about it. All I can say is that it's been a great source of inspiration in resolving things."

The Zen teaching that Wiley encountered in San Francisco was essentially that of Shunryu Suzuki, founder of the Zen Center and author of *Zen Mind, Beginner's Mind,* from which the quotation at the beginning of this essay is taken. As the title suggests, Suzuki's writings emphasize a constant return to basics and minimize the significance of attempting to achieve Enlightenment. If Enlightenment is to come, he says, it is more likely to do so through careful attention to routine, by concentrating on each action and extracting from it as much as possible. Suzuki says, "Zen is not some kind of excitement, but concentration on our usual, everyday routine."[3]

Wiley's easy going demeanor is matched by a strong personal discipline. He works at his studio regularly, whether he feels like painting that day or not, and on occasion forces himself to work in ways seemingly alien to his normal procedures. When that happens, the results can be startling. For example, having set himself to color in a grid—to make a painting as much like an Ellsworth Kelly as anything else—Wiley completed it with one of the squares showing a small piece of earth with sprouting grass. Implicitly, the question is raised: do the other squares conceal small sections of earth—or sky, or water? And if what is under each square were revealed, would a complete landscape be uncovered?

---

3. Shunryu Suzuki
Zen Mind, Beginner's Mind
New York: John Weatherhill, Inc., 1977, p 57.

Wiley's little riddle is closely related to a Zen concept of the potential of any given form—the simpler the form, the more interpretations it can bear and, correspondingly, the more evolved the form, the simpler it will be. Each of the squares in Wiley's painting can become what the onlooker wants it to be. Beneath the colored grid Wiley has written, "I wish I could have known earlier that you have all the time you'll ever need right up to the day you die." A reminder that, in Wiley's opinion, every moment contains the seeds of fulfillment. The statement is almost pure Suzuki. In fact, Wiley's statement serves the purpose of a koan, a question and answer technique used in Zen teaching to stimulate creative thought. To westerners, the most notable feature of a koan is its stark illogicality, and a question such as "What is the sound of one hand clapping?" is self-contradictory. A koan is intended to remind the intellect that it too has its limitations. As one Zen sage wrote, "A psychological impasse is the necessary antecedent to Enlightenment... The worst enemy of the Zen experience, at least in the beginning, is the intellect."[4] The verbal statement in Wiley's watercolor, though capable of some intuitive interpretation, cannot be fully explained in relation to the visual image. Rather, it acts as a stimulus to contemplation of the cryptic little squares.

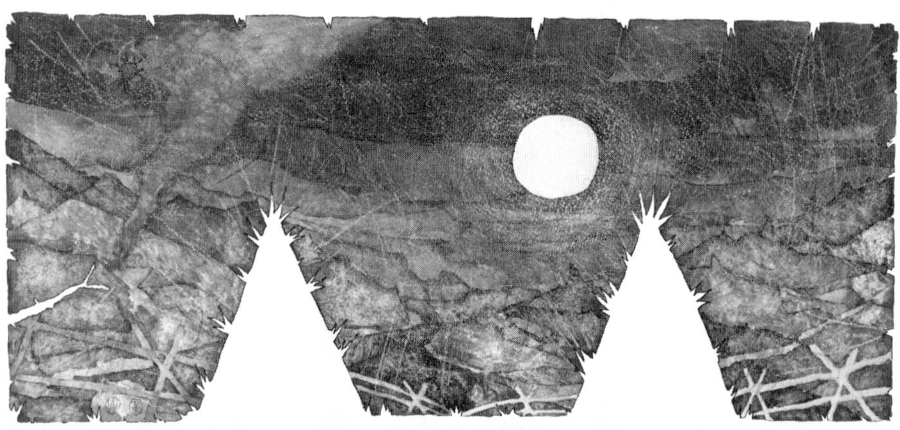

Where the Scare Grows 1976
watercolor and ink on paper
22 x 30
Courtesy Hansen Fuller Goldeen Gallery
San Francisco

4. D. T. Suzuki
Zen Buddhism, Selected Writings of D. T. Suzuki
ed. William Barrett
Garden City, New York: Doubleday & Company, Inc., 1956, pp 136-7.

Mr. Nobody 1973
acrylic and charcoal on canvas
80 x 47½
Collection Wally Goodman and Stan Picher
San Francisco

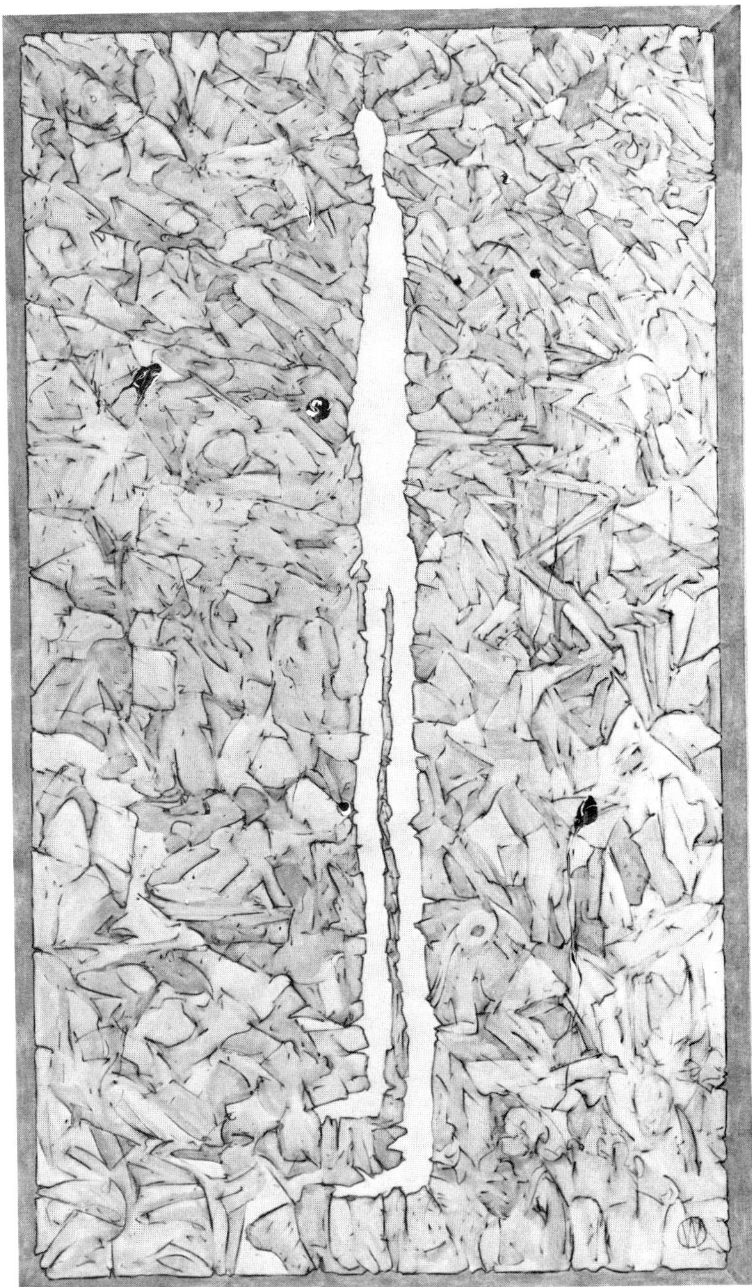

Certain of Wiley's pictorial devices that recur throughout his work are variations of other Zen attitudes. The empty spaces of *Where the Scare Grows*, 1976, or *Mr. Nobody*, 1973, refer to the related concepts of "No mind," and "Form is void." Zen emphasis on maintaining a proper mental attitude, notably one of watchful respect, is reflected in the titles of various works, such as the watercolor *Hide as a State of Mind*, 1971. Similarly, the title of the 1970-71 work, *Thank You Hide*, echoes teachings that sources of inspiration should be gratefully acknowledged. Above all, Zen taught Wiley a lesson, reinforced by his own experience—to accept things as they come and seek further meaning in them, rather than cast them aside as "finished" or "understood."

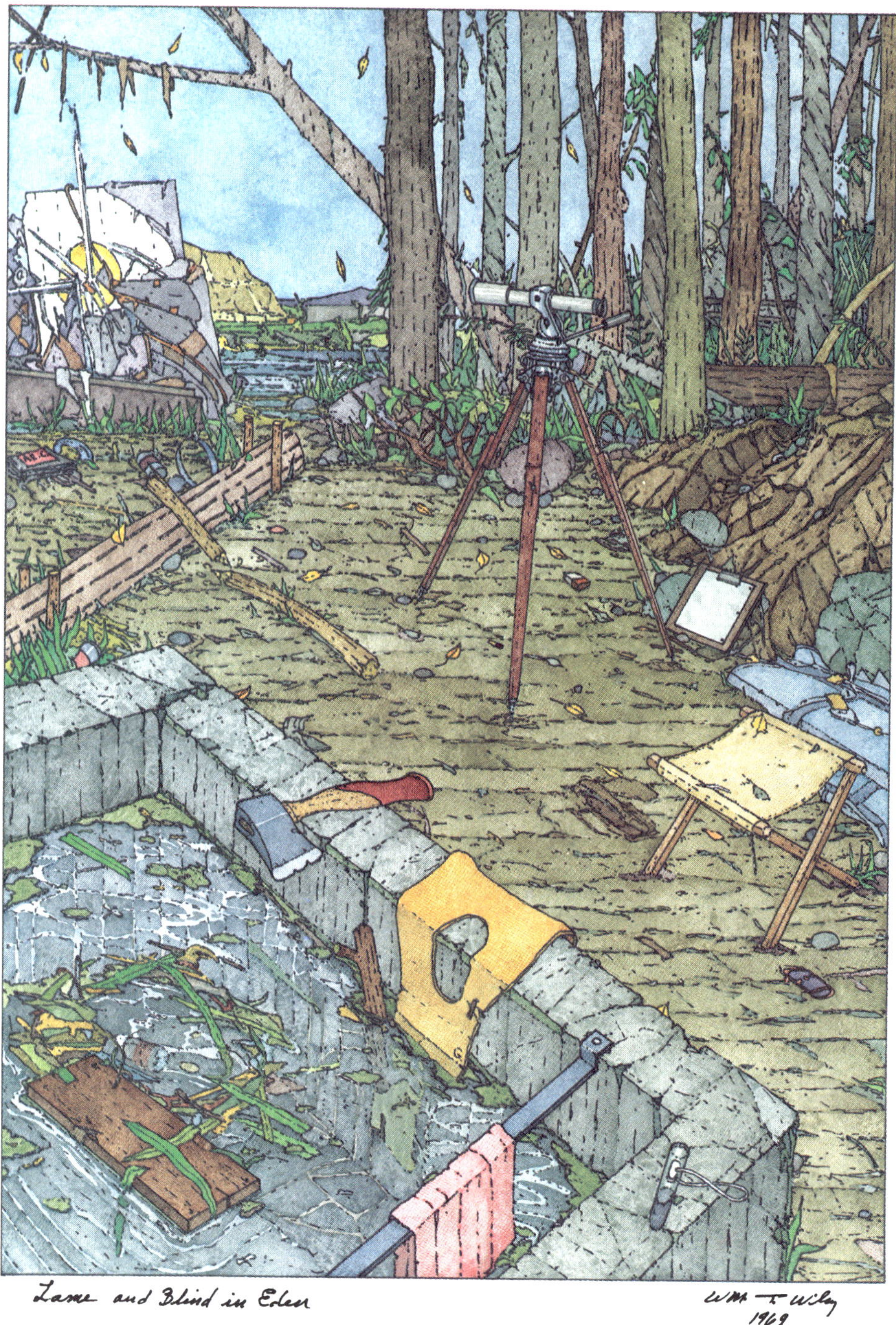

Lame and Blind in Eden 1969
watercolor and ink on paper
30 x 22
Collection Mr. and Mrs. Harry W. Anderson
Atherton, California

I have borrowed my adjectives from the Greeks, who developed their mystical doctrines of art through plausible embodiments, not through purely conceptual means.

Frederich Nietzsche, *The Birth of Tragedy*

Metaphor, the substitution of one object or idea for another to achieve dramatic or poetic emphasis, lies at the center of Wiley's art. By consistent, imaginative use of carefully selected images, Wiley has given new meaning to such venerable symbols as triangles and figure eights, and revitalized the old themes concerning wayfaring, magic and the court jester/wise fool. By this process he has found a unique vehicle for expressing his attitudes towards life.

Wiley's symbols fall into two basic categories—the abstract and the realistic. His most common abstract symbols are the triangle, the figure eight/infinity symbol, the tic-tac-toe mark and the black and white strip. They frequently overlap and coalesce with each other and with the realistic group that includes knives, hatchets, logs, skins, lightning bolts, maps, moons, boats and dunce caps.

Although Wiley's symbology is intricate and personal, he can provide explanations for individual elements. Sometimes an explanation is illuminating, at other times it is confounding. A question, for example, about the source of his ubiquitous triangle—ancient symbol of power and basic concept of Western rationalist thought—can evoke an honest, if not entirely satisfactory, response about a childhood visit to a chiropractor where he saw a drawing of a triangle on the office wall with the words, "God," "Patient," "Chiropractor," written, one at each corner. A true conjurer, Wiley is careful to maintain the mystery of his symbols. A more formal explanation of the triangle's appearance in his work is its use as a simple compositional element in his earlier expressionist paintings. Most of all, its shape is pleasing to him. He uses it as a device to begin a work of art, in much the same way that a koan stimulates a train of thought.

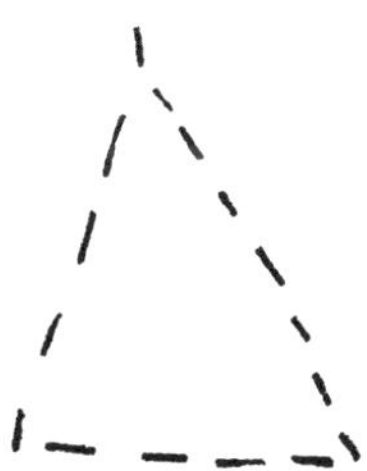

A triangular structure underlies the 1973 watercolor, *What's Left of the Garden and Mirror,* ostensibly a simple view of the yard behind the artist's studio. The shape of the mirror, a triangular one that Wiley once owned, is echoed by the garden borders and by other planks propped up against the fence. A delicate network of red triangles that forms a screen between the viewer and the garden emanates from a denser, but still transparent, barrier at the bottom of the drawing. Wiley has imbued the scene with the quality of a dream. This lyrical, green-gray painting, fusing the descriptive with the metaphysical, exemplifies Wiley's matter-of-fact mysticism.

What's Left of the Garden and Mirror 1973
watercolor, ink and colored pencil on paper
30 x 22
Collection Mr. and Mrs. C. David Robinson
Sausalito, California

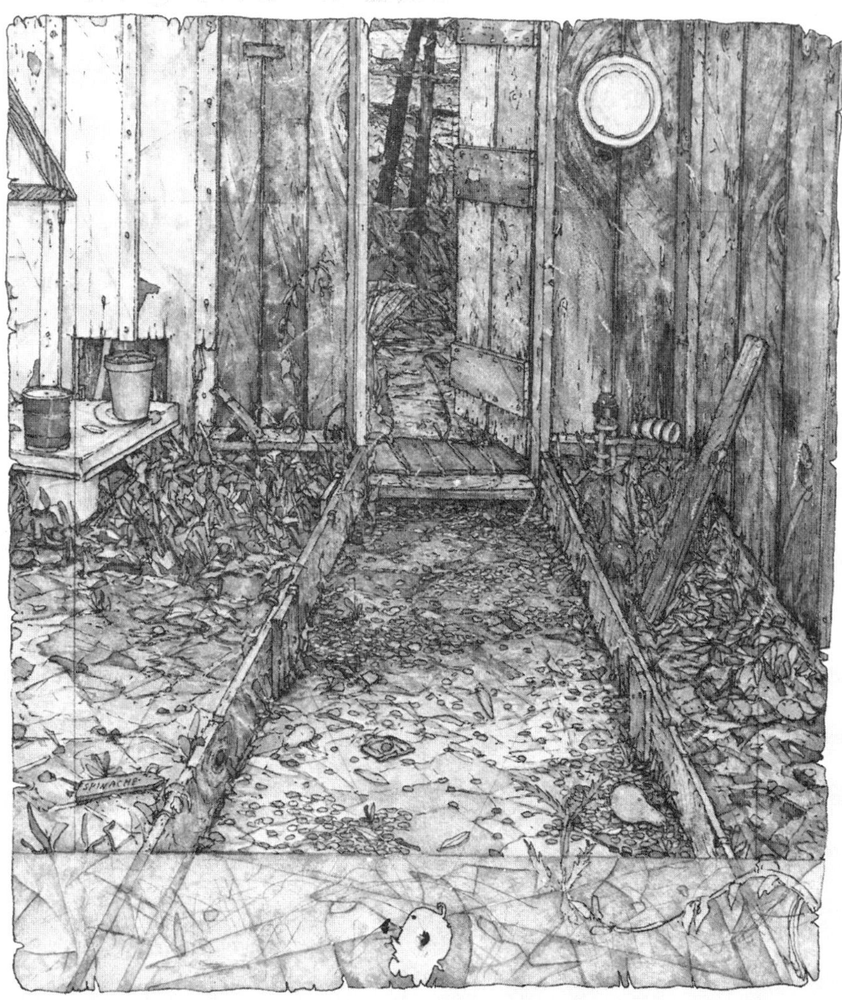

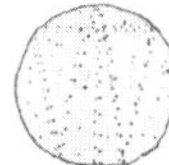

Combined with the circle, the triangle becomes the cone, or in Wiley's hands, the wizard's hat or dunce's cap that adorns Mr. Unatural in all his appearances. In the 1973 watercolor, *Certain Things No One Can Teach You,* cone and triangle combine to create a hybrid form, a section of a circle.

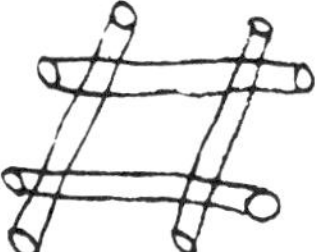

The banal tic-tac-toe mark, initially included as a reference to Westermann's work, has taken on many meanings for Wiley. He sees the four elements as referring to his wife, his two sons and himself. Other meanings gradually accrued: "I saw it in a typesetting box and (was told) it's used in typesetting to indicate space; it's a symbol that you want space there. And in the *I Ching,* the same mark occurs—I think it's innocence. It's also a scuffle mark. I've never felt very pushed to press into why a shape is there or where it comes from. I use it, it overlaps with something else and I find a history of references."

Certain Things No One Can Teach You 1973
watercolor, ink and acrylic on paper
22 x 30
Collection Diana Fuller
San Francisco

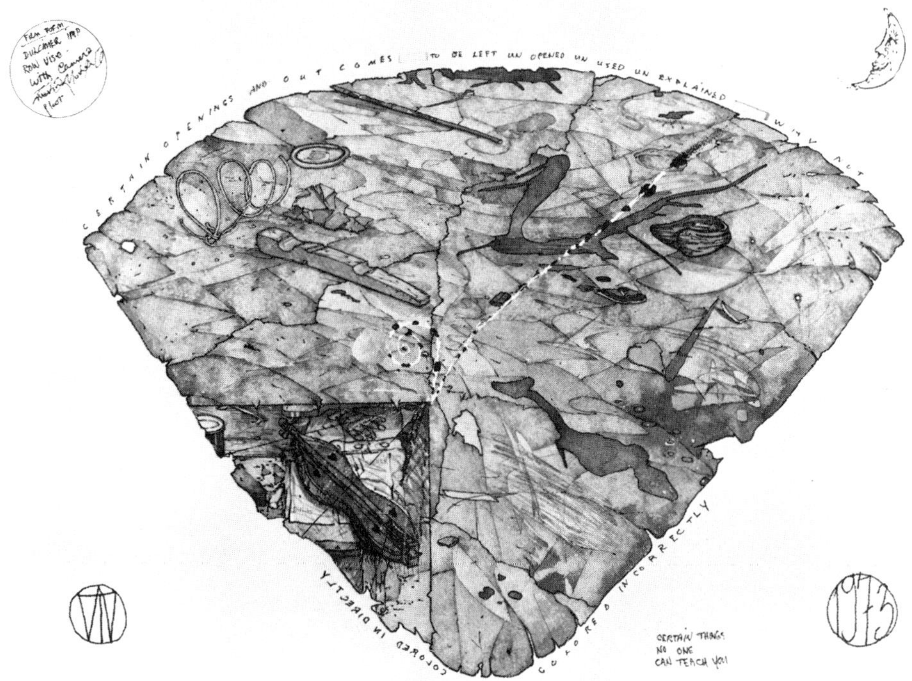

First Stage of Infinity 1971
construction of wood, leather, twisted branches and ink on cloth
23½ x 22 x 3¾
Courtesy Allan Frumkin Gallery
New York

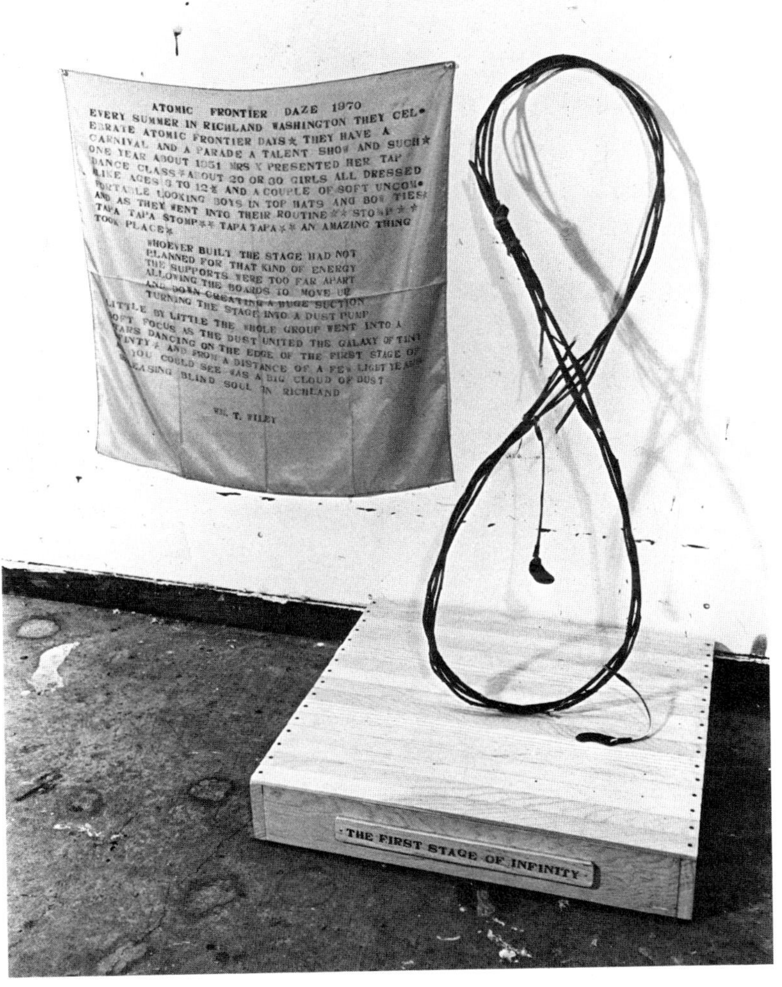

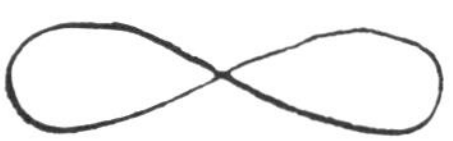

Wiley's relatively specific ideas about life and death include belief in reincarnation. The infinity symbol—an abstract version of a mythological beast that everlastingly grows by consuming its own tail—frequently appears in his work as, he says, "a reminder." The figure eight stands as a sculpture of intertwined twigs in the 1971 work, *First Stage of Infinity.* Behind the symbol hangs a scarf bearing a narrative describing a mishap at a yearly festival honoring the nuclear power plant in Richland, Washington, where Wiley grew up. From the event, humorous and trivial at a time when nuclear power was generally regarded with optimism, Wiley extracts a sinister message. The figure eight, made of hedge clippings, becomes a contemporary crown of thorns. In *Bridge for Trudy,* a sharply focused 1969 watercolor that deals with the impending death of a terminally ill friend, the infinity symbol occurs in each corner, twice overtly, twice in disguised form. In this drawing, a stream is intersected by a strange, white cloth barrier, a rendering of a sculpture that Bill Allan and Bruce Nauman constructed at Muir Creek. The fresh green grass on the "far" bank contrasts with the bare earth on the near one. Partly obscuring this arid patch is a pale, simplified sketch of the whole drawing. The symbolism is direct: Wiley suggests that life in this world is an insignificant part of a greater chain of existence.

Bridge for Trudy 1969
watercolor and ink on paper
21 x 29
Collection Carl E. Horn
Summit, New Jersey

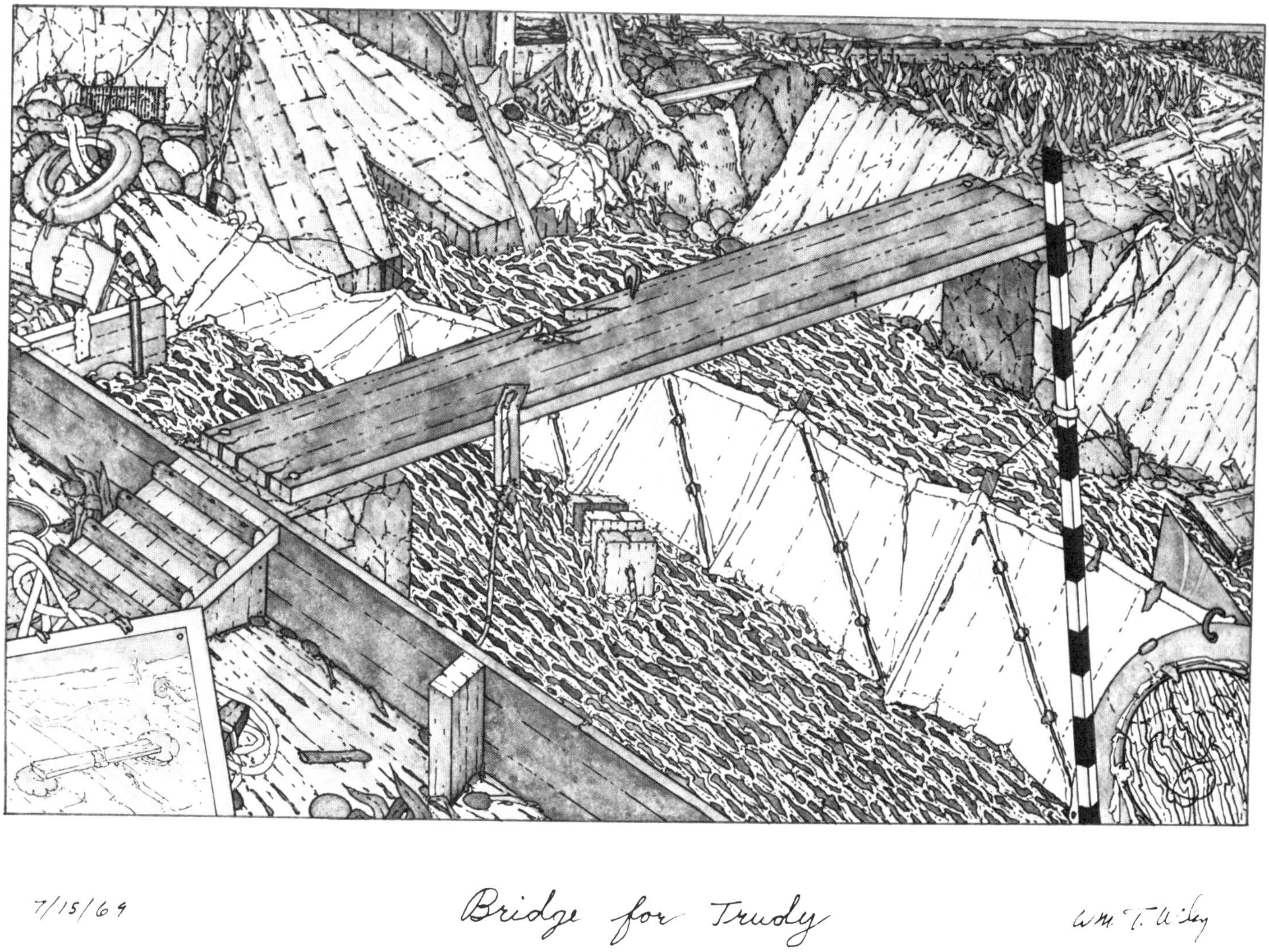

7/15/69 Bridge for Trudy Wm T. Wiley

Wizdumb Bridge 1969
watercolor and ink on paper
24 x 19
Collection William and Deborah Struve
Chicago

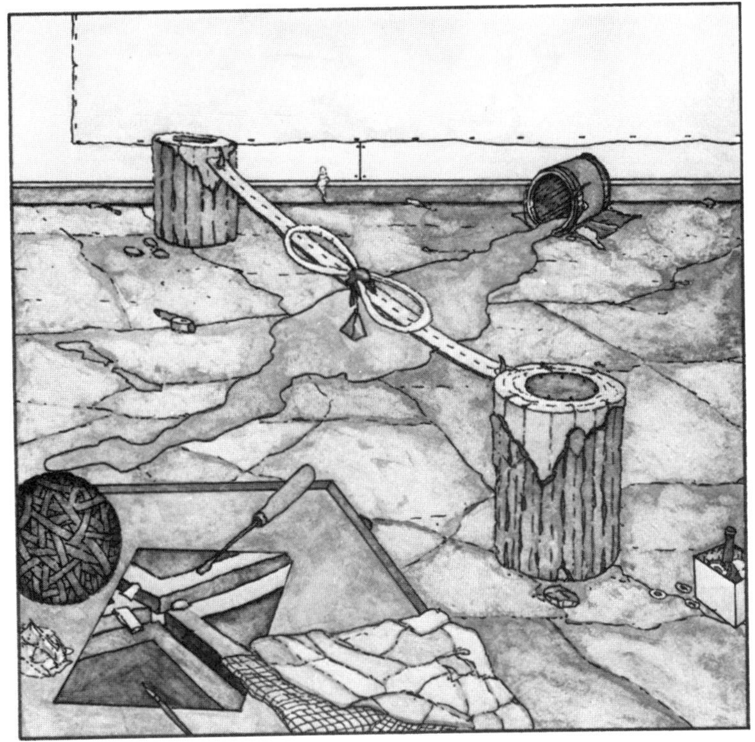

Wizdumb Bridge

I'm a maze of information about reflections, mirrored in opposites. Dad's tool box always contained an instrument which i could never define a purpose for. Dad wasn't crippled in any way i could see at that time, yet the tool that didn't seem to fit was in there with the others laying like a brace for some unrealized disease.

Wm. T. Wiley
7/10/69

As a child, Wiley was fascinated by the collection of instruments his father used during a brief career as a surveyor. Best of all he liked those whose functions were obscure. Included in the 1969 watercolor, *Wizdumb Bridge*, is the statement, "Dad's toolbox always contained an instrument which I could never define a purpose for. Dad wasn't crippled in any way I could see at that time. Yet, the tool that didn't seem to fit was in there with the others, laying like a brace for some unrealized disease." The black and white staff—called a picket or range pole—is a familiar implement of the surveyor, used as an aid in taking measurements over long distances. Wiley "loved the way it looked, that black and white staff in a big green field or against the woods," and exploits this dramatic contrast in the vivid 1971-72 watercolor, *Land Escape*, which consists of a brilliant green abstract landscape intersected by two vertical range poles. The staff appears as a sculptural element in the 1971 painting and construction *Random Remarks and Digs*, where it pins a wooden triangle to the painting. Elsewhere, it is combined with other familiar signs—for example, the tic-tac-toe mark in *I Won't Forget Again One Jillion Times*, a large, gray painting of 1973 that is almost completely abstract. In *Painting for Rain* of 1976, the black and white strip is transformed into a spiral—a schematic whirlpool superimposed on an arid, ochre landscape—a charm invoked by the artist to break the 1976 drought that caused such damage in California.

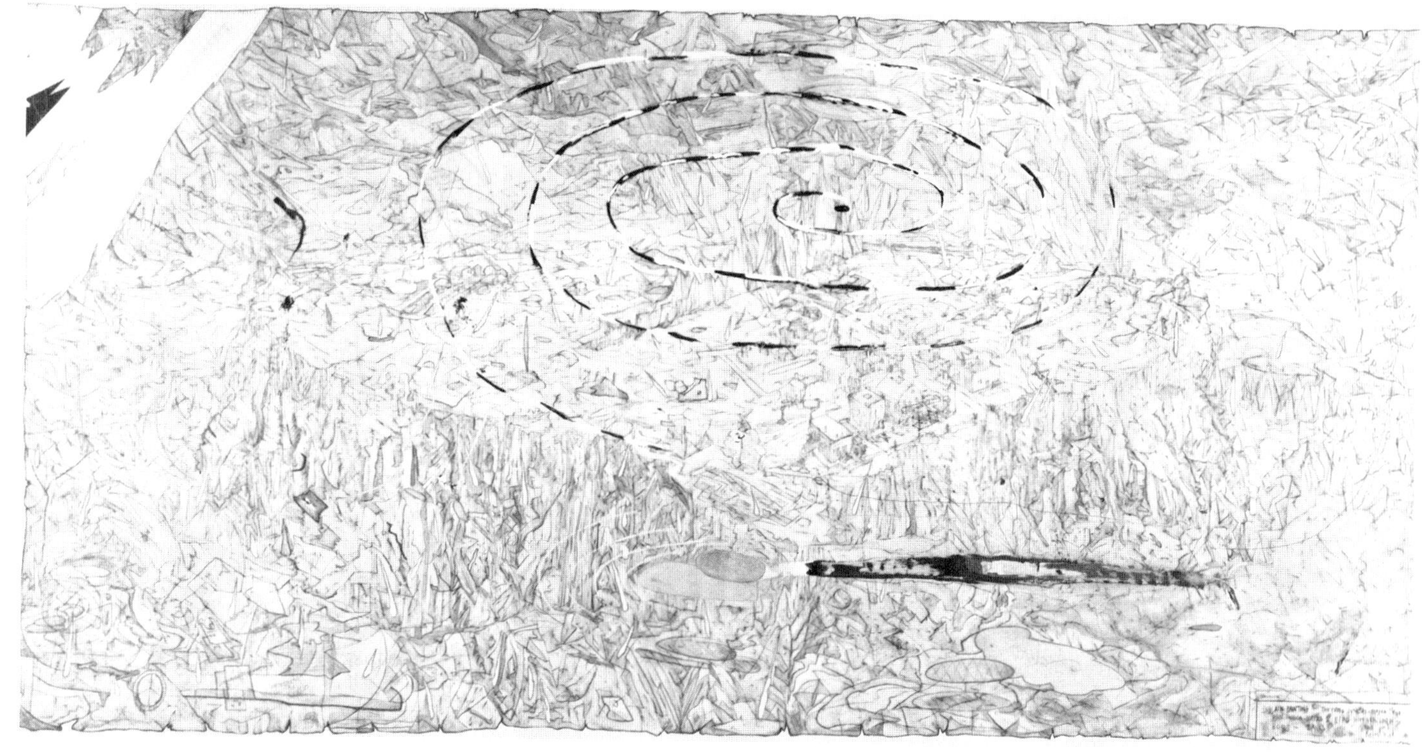

Painting for Rain 1976
acrylic and chalk on canvas
93 x 183
Collection Dallas Museum of Fine Arts
Foundation for the Arts Collection
Anonymous gift in memory of
Edward S. Marcus

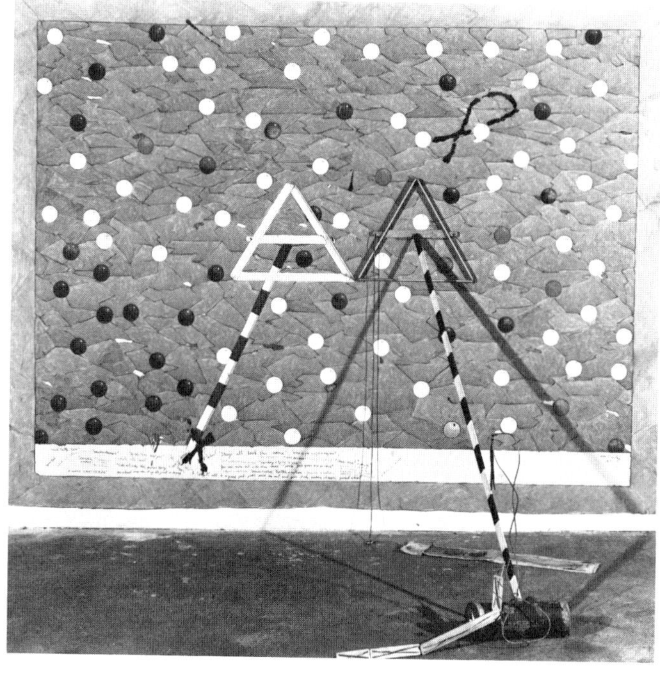

Random Remarks and Digs 1971
painting of acrylic on canvas
86 x 115 x 40 (irregular)
construction of wood, metal and cloth
Collection Mr. and Mrs. C. David Robinson
Sausalito, California

Land Escape 1971-72
watercolor and ink on paper
22 x 30
Collection Goldyne Family
San Francisco

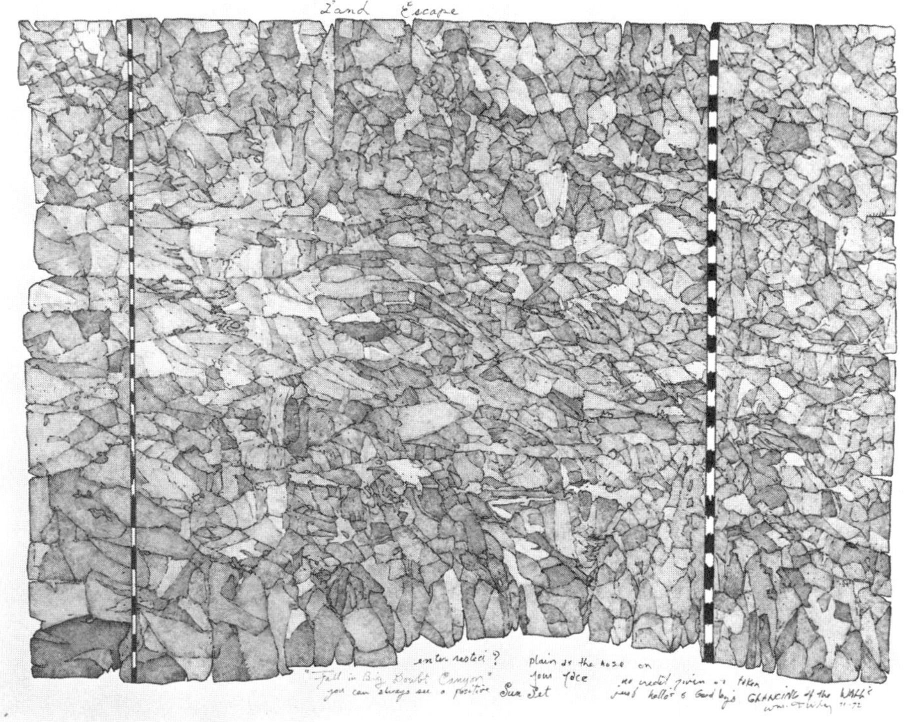

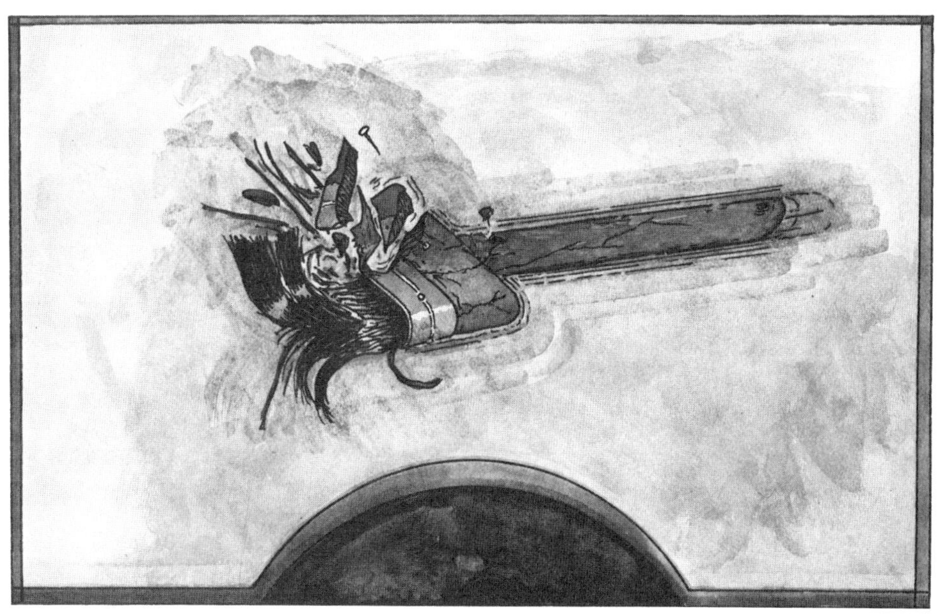

Brush exploding in Space
1967

Brush Exploding in Space 1967
watercolor and ink on paper
18 x 24
Private Collection, New York

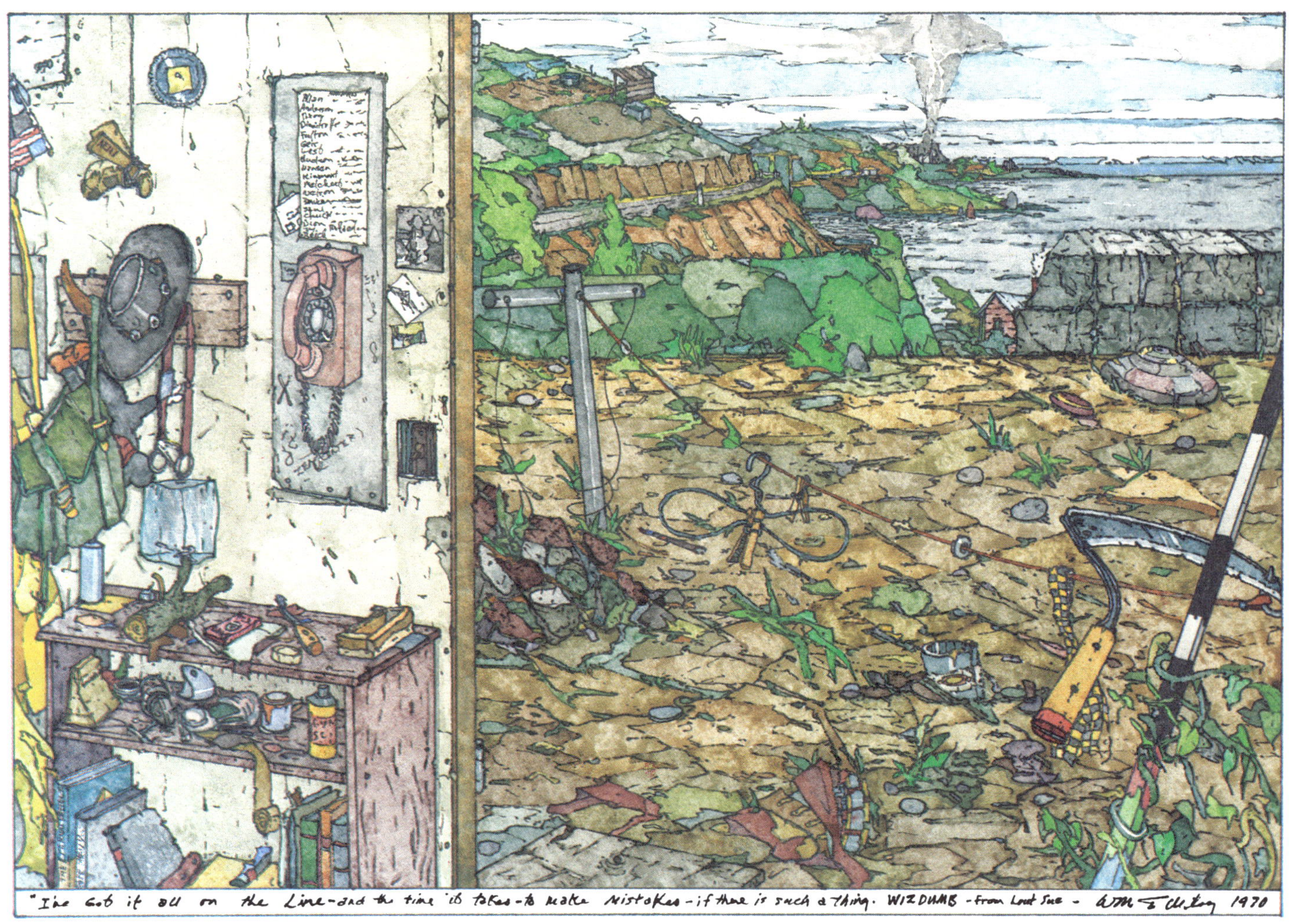

I've Got it All on the Line 1970
watercolor and ink on paper
22 x 30
Courtesy Odyssia Gallery
New York

In *Hide As A State of Mind,* the strip not only intersects the landscape—an abstract version of the United States—it acts as a barrier to the color. The "land" to the left of the strip is fully painted, that to the right is left unfinished. The suspicion that the strip is Wiley's magic wand is confirmed by its subsequent appearance as the forked staff of Wiley's wise-fool, Mr. Unatural, one of several alter ego figures dealt with later in this essay.

Alongside these symbols recurs a group of objects from Wiley's immediate surroundings, notably his studio where he often begins a work by drawing what he sees in front of him. This free association approach suggests ideas and directions that, in turn, affect the final appearance of the selected object. The watercolor, *Brush Exploding in Space,* began as a simple rendition of a brush on the studio table. As the drawing progressed, Wiley made one of those unaccountable connections that characterize his approach. He thought of Constantin Brancusi's exquisite abstract sculpture, *Bird in Space,* and decided to imbue his brush with properties of flight. In a further, perverse step, he made the brush explode, thus opposing the erupting force of his drawing to the consummately controlled energy implied in Brancusi's sculpture.

Sometimes Wiley's leaps of imagination bring together quite separate locations in his imagery. The cluttered landscape of the 1970 watercolor, *I've Got it All On the Line,* started out as a straight studio view—"the telephone, things that were hanging there at the time. I got over to the door that was closed. I decided that was too dull so I opened the door... and saw the sickle hanging on the fence. I decided a broken down rock wall would be more interesting than a fence... that it would be much nicer to have a studio closer to the ocean. The view is based on a section of the coast over near Muir Beach where we used to go fishing... I just hauled the coast in."

From the clothesline that runs across the foreground of the landscape is suspended a clothes hanger in the by now familiar infinity symbol shape, and on a hook at the edge of the painting at an improbable angle hangs a sickle. The sickle blade is notched, as are those of the hatchets, knives and razors in other Wiley paintings. The dangerous implement (a personification of death?) is itself impaired.

The disparate sources for the two parts of *I've Got it All on the Line,* are not quite reconciled and the relationship of studio wall to landscape is strange—almost as if they were two separate stage sets, one trying to push the other aside. What began as a mundane view of a wall that Wiley encounters daily, evolved into a surrealist essay exploring dislocated space and time, reminiscent of de Chirico's 1917 painting, *The Great Metaphysician.*

Simple, man-made implements, in Wiley's translations can be powerful metaphors for frightening and destructive machines. In the poignant watercolor, *Lame and Blind in Eden,* Wiley's theme was the inevitable corruption and decay that man brings to any new land, particularly one he calls "Paradise." Eden is California, and Wiley is reacting to the massive visual and physical pollution that has occurred there in the last 20 years. The danger of nuclear power is something he feels particularly strongly about, but no steaming nuclear plants are evident in *Lame and Blind in Eden.* Instead, use-worn implements litter the foreground. A notched axe, tattered folding stool, discarded clip board and test tube are among the recognizable detritus scattered around a crumbling, square concrete pool. An abandoned telescope points beyond a ravaged copse and pile of junk to distant, as yet untouched, hills.

Hidden in the realistically drawn implements of *Lame and Blind in Eden* are Wiley's abstract symbols. The clamp attached to the test tube is in a figure eight configuration. The crossed struts of the folding chair comprise a hatchmark, and the legs of the telescope tripod delineate a pyramid. Missing is the familiar black and white striped pole. Perhaps the magic wand is powerless in the face of such destruction.

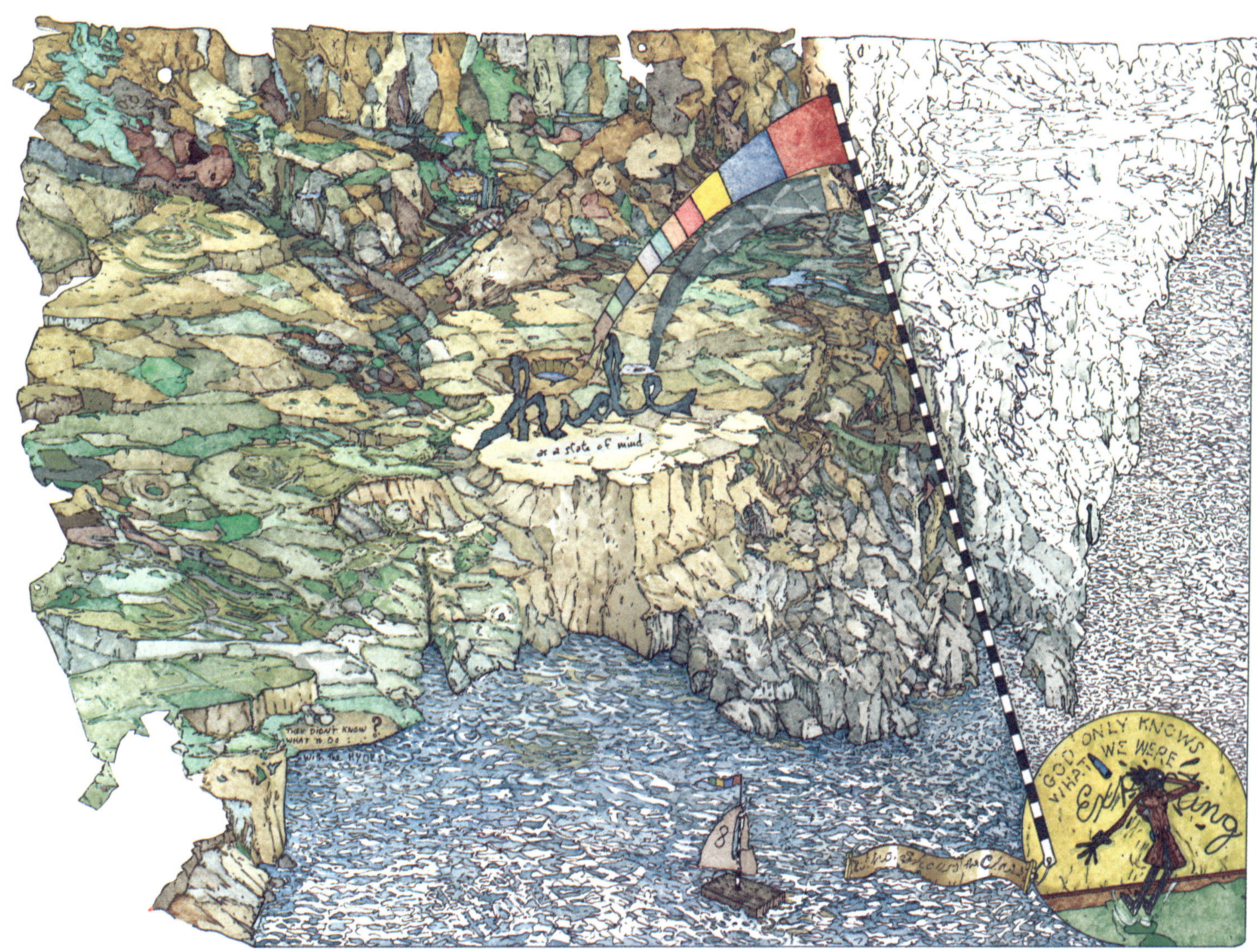

Hide as a State of Mind 1971
ink and watercolor on paper
22 x 30
Collection Des Moines Art Center
Dr. Maurice H. Noun Bequest Fund, 1971

...let me go on, and tell my story in my own way—if I should seem now and then to trifle upon the road, or should sometimes put on a fool's cap with a bell on it for a moment or two, don't fly off, but rather give me credit for a little more wisdom than appears on my outside—and as we jogg on, either laugh with me or at me or, in short, do anything—only keep your temper.

Laurence Sterne, *Tristram Shandy*

Wiley's ubiquitous symbols are woven into a number of distinct but related recurring themes: wayfaring by land and sea, the West, magic and Wiley's own art. Bizarre though some of these may seem, they all derive from Wiley's own lifestyle and activities.

How to Chart a Coarse

Wiley's home in Marin County is not very far from the sea, or from the "Big Sky" country of the great West. Of all his themes, he has invested the metaphor of travel as life cycle with unexpected vitality. Maps, schematic representations of vast spaces themselves, fascinate him and are a constant source of inspiration. "There's a map I saw in Europe on my way to the Sistine Chapel... a really old map of the world collaged together... It was such a raw, first hand impression, you could see how people thought of the world then."[5] *Village Roots*, 1972, a large, elegant painting, is an abstract visualization of the handful of towns he has lived in. His father's search for a good living took Wiley from Indiana to Texas to Washington state. Wiley's final move was to California when, as a student, he went to San Francisco. The painting features craggy, low relief terrain that, like ancient maps, shows geographic features from inconsistent viewpoints, some subjects being seen from the side, some from above. The edge of the painting, as is invariably the case, is ragged and tattered like an old chart or map drawn on leather.

References to a shadowy character called Nomad—the quintessential wayfarer—crop up in works of the early 70s. "Nomad," Wiley tells us, "is an island." The name is borrowed, again from Westermann, but in his translation the phrase is a punning reference to John Donne's line from *Devotions*, "No man is an *island* entire of itself." Wiley agrees with Donne and sees Nomad as being condemned to a life of wandering, cast adrift to comment on the world through which he makes his lonely way.

---

5. Dan Tooker
"How to Chart a Course:
An Interview with William T. Wiley"
Artscanada, Spring 1974, p 84.

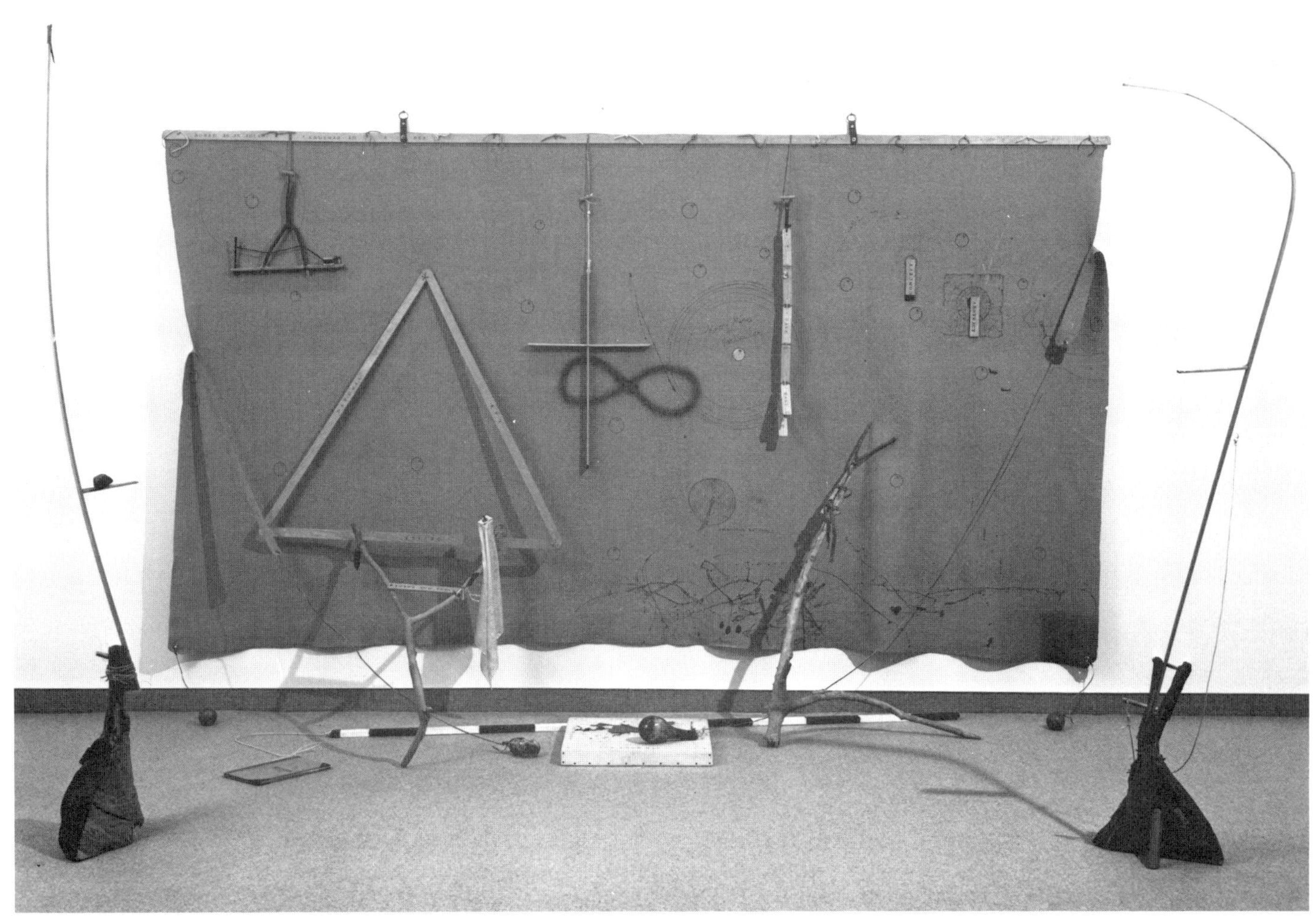

How to Chart a Coarse 1971
construction of acrylic and ink on felt, leather, painted wood, wire, brass, branches, glass, silk, ink on canvas, rubber, metal, hard-bound book and rabbits' feet
87 x 144 x 78
two drawings of watercolor and ink on paper
30 x 22 each
Collection Ralph H. Perkins and Steven Smith
Chicago

The imagery for much of Wiley's travel is nautical. In the early construction, *Ship's Log*, 1969, a large, elaborate arrangement of poles, spars, ropes, cinches and a triangular sail-like piece of canvas, hang behind a diminutive book—the ship's log—describing the process of making a work, a "journey" of the mind. By the kind of coincidence that Wiley welcomes, the old fashioned ship's log used for estimating speed was triangular in shape. *Dried Ox-Bow Trail*, the title of a 1972 watercolor, is a pun—"Dry Docks—Boat Rail"—and the general wayfaring reference of the first reading gives way to a second, specifically nautical one. In this work, a little steamboat lies embedded in dry mud and a spectral, not quite funny, wire figure stalks across the parched landscape. The same wire figure appears as a harpoonist alongside some whale-like shapes in the construction elements of *Village Roots*. Wiley is drawing upon associations with the ultimate American naturalistic-symbolist novel, *Moby Dick*, by Herman Melville.

Ship's Log 1969
construction of canvas, leather, wood, lead, paper, ink, watercolor, cotton webbing, latex rubber, plastic, salt licks, wire, nautical hardware and assorted hardware
82 x 78 x 54
Collection San Francisco Museum of Modern Art
Gerstle Fund Purchase

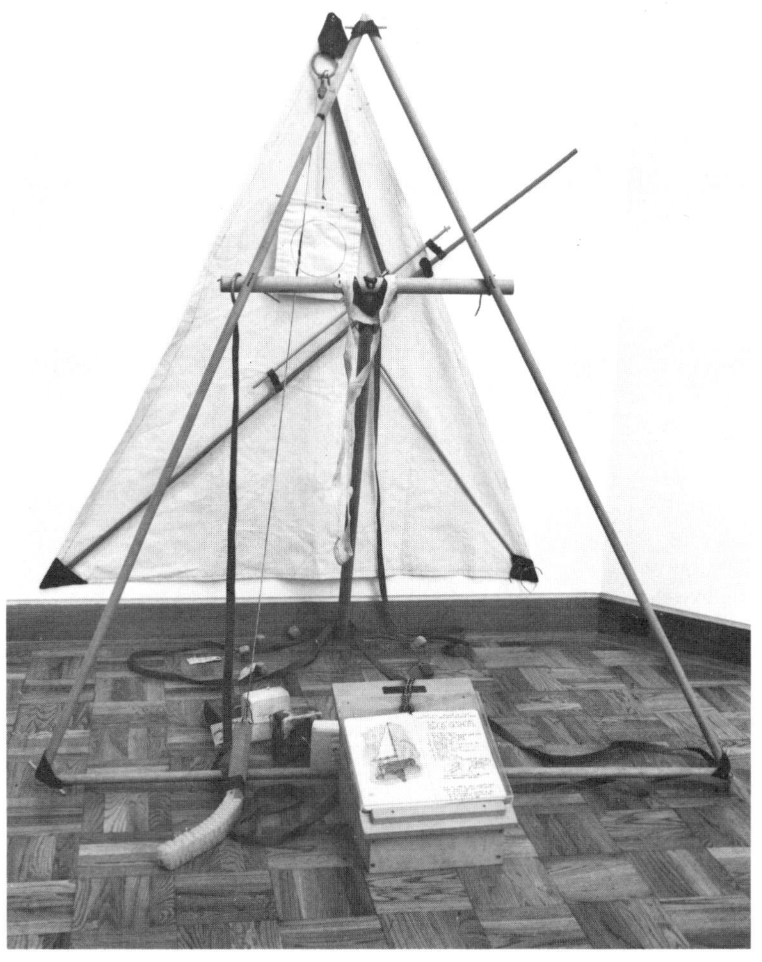

Dried Ox-Bow Trail 1972
watercolor and ink on paper
22 x 30
Collection San Francisco Museum of Modern Art
Gift of the Women's Board

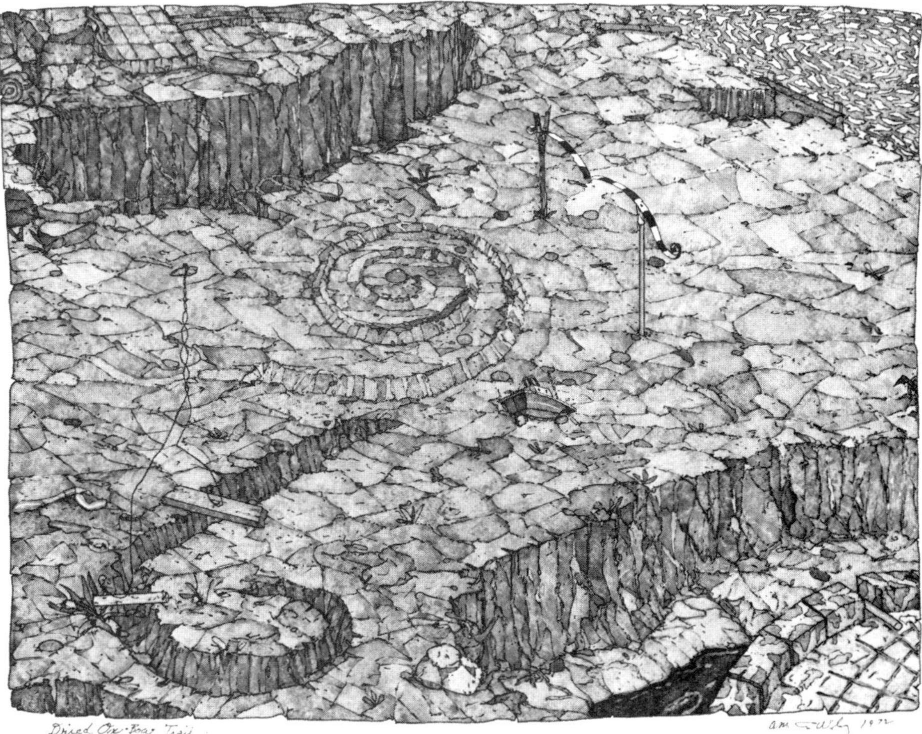

Village Roots 1972
painting of acrylic on canvas
96 x 156
two constructions of wood, metal and wire
17 x 25 x 3½; 4 x 25 x 3½
Collection Los Angeles County Museum of Art
Purchased with matching funds of the National Endowment for the Arts and the Modern and Contemporary Art Council

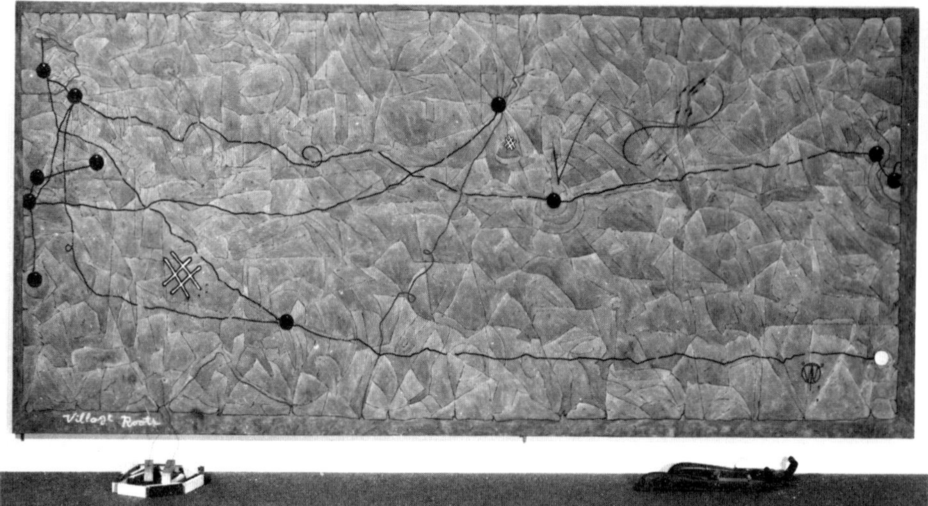

A misleadingly helpful sounding title, *How to Chart a Coarse*, accompanies a 1971 construction. An expanded version of *Ship's Log*, it contains virtually all of Wiley's favorite symbols but, contrary to what the tale leads us to expect, no explanation is provided. Like the objects in his father's toolbox, the purpose or function of each element has to be imagined. *How to Chart a Coarse* is not so much a lesson in navigation as an invitation to alchemy.

Wiley's most extensive, and disturbing, utilization of the nautical theme occurs in the four-part work, *The Hound Harbor Series*, of 1977. The landscape depicted in its largest component, a painting, is more resolved than previous treatments of such themes, but the resolution is not comforting. Skeletal fragments abound and tall buildings rise out of a hostile looking terrain in a manner reminiscent of Hieronymus Bosch's scenes of hell. The triangular construction that sits in front of the painting resembles a boat that, paradoxically, seems to be made of flotsam and jetsam. Imbedded in the construction is the legend, "Mark my words, Lady. You've not sailed with the likes of Captain Nobody." In a smaller painting, Captain Nobody is revealed to us as the figure of death, a skeleton in sailor's clothes. Wiley remains vague about his titles. Too complete an explanation, he feels, closes off too many lines of speculation. "I have," Wiley says, "no idea where the name (Hound Harbor) came from... I might have been hounded at the time."

There is no doubt of Wiley's candor in these matters and, as we have seen, a simple association is frequently the starting point for an elaborate work of art. Anything can set him off and it is quite conceivable that a temporary urge to seek a haven from being pursued (by whom Wiley cannot remember) was enough to generate a major construction. Nevertheless, Wiley's instincts for the telling phrase are uncanny and his choice of title—if we allow ourselves to indulge in a little speculation—can evoke recollections of the mythological Cerberus, hound of the Underworld.

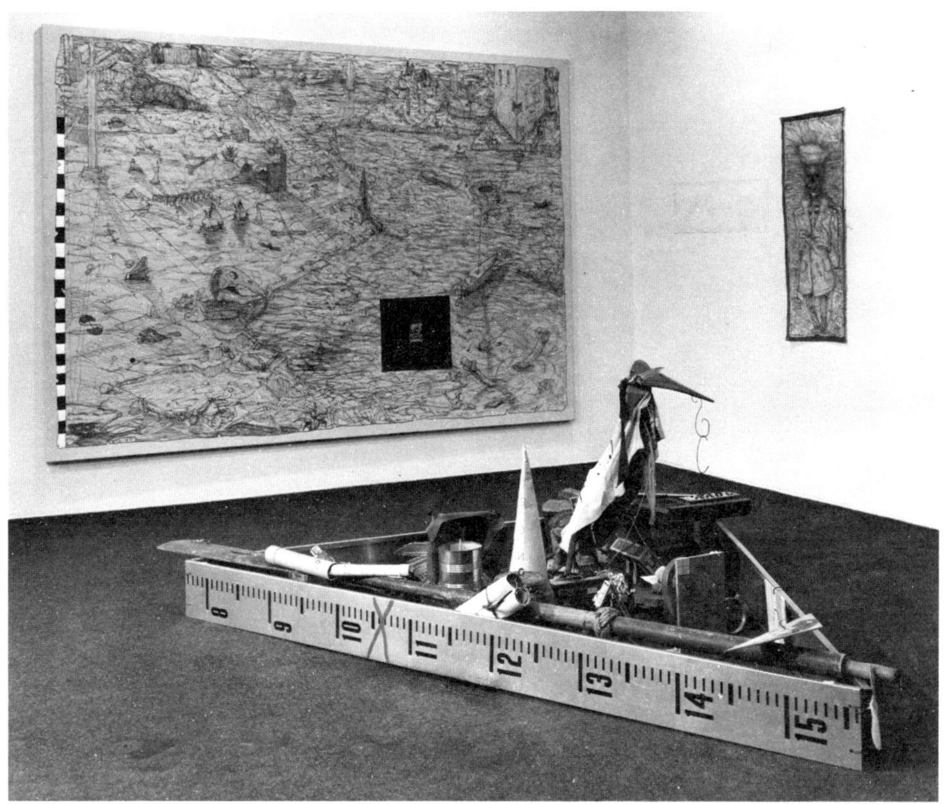

The Hound Harbor Series 1977
construction of aluminum, wood, metal, acrylic
and charcoal on canvas, nylon, plastic, vinyl,
leather, watercolor on paper, feathers, tin,
masonite, acrylic on chamois hide, paper
and found objects
25 x 96 x 93
painting of pastel on unstretched canvas
42¼ x 18½
painting of acrylic and ink on stretched canvas
78¾ x 115
drawing of charcoal on parchment
30 x 41
Collection Denver Art Museum
National Endowment for the Arts Purchase Fund
and Volunteer Benefits Fund

Dude ranches flourish in Marin County, but Wiley has not exploited western themes as thoroughly as nautical ones. No lonesome cowboys plod their weary way through his work and no sinister bad guys appear as counterparts to the dreadful Captain Nobody. The cowboy hat that appears in some of the watercolors is Wiley's own. "I used to wear it more than I do now," he says. The imposingly traditional Winchester rifle, is a mere .22, purchased to eliminate the ground squirrels decimating his wife's garden. For all the apparently leather stocking accoutrements—buck knives, log cabins and axes—Wiley's West derives from his own back yard and his vacation house in the mountains. The western flavor is strongest in the short poems written beneath the watercolors, some of which read like sad trail songs. Some titles—*Meditating at Fort Prank, Frontier Baptism Camp,* evoke visions of early settlers in the old West, but the pioneering that Wiley suggests is more of a spiritual than historical nature.

Thank You Hide 1970-71
construction of wood, leather, ink and charcoal on cowhide, pickaxe, found objects
70 x 64
six drawings of watercolor and ink on paper
1 drawing, 16 x 12; 5 drawings, 12 x 16
Collection Des Moines Art Center
Coffin Fine Arts Trust Fund, 1977

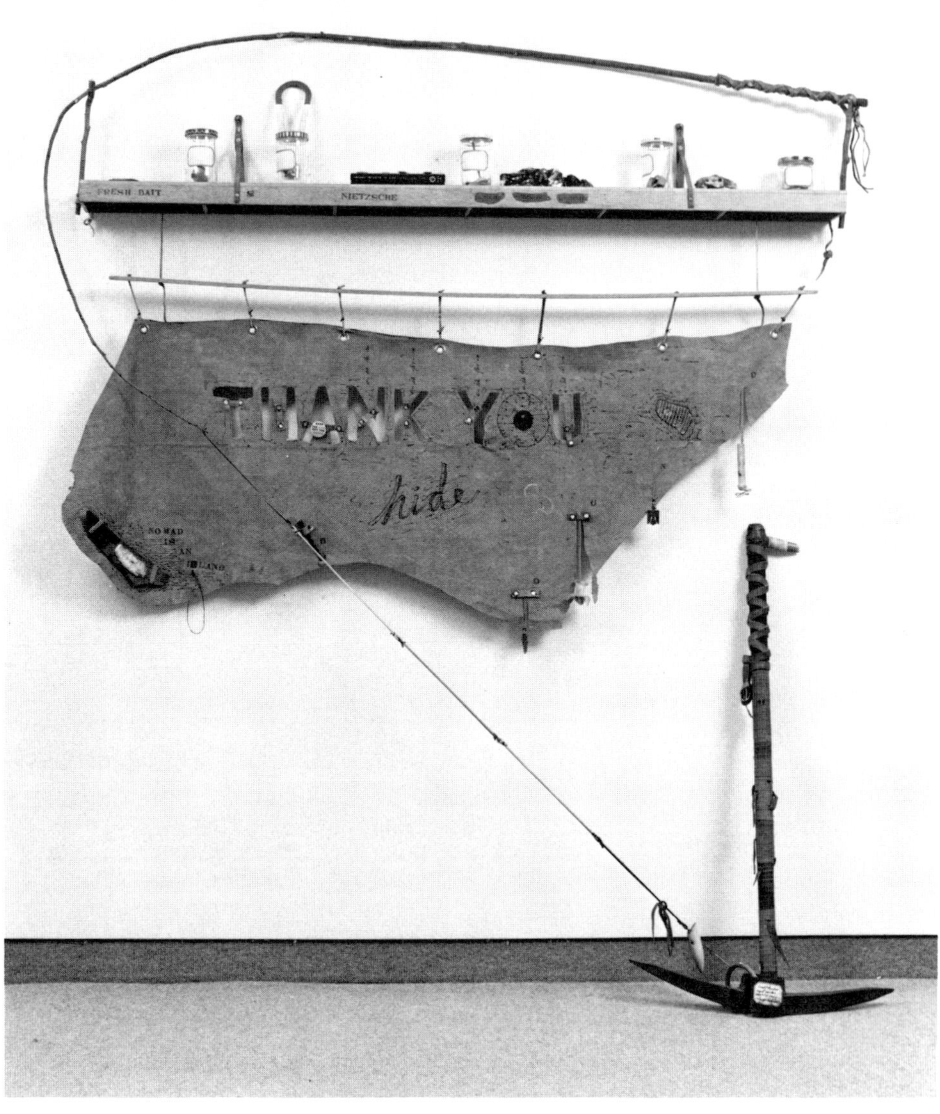

Thank You Hide

The potent, ancient art of American Indians holds more fascination for Wiley than the tales and objects associated with the white man's West. A number of free-standing constructions—*It Remains to be Seen*, for example—resemble worm-eaten totems and fetishes. In this liberal use of materials, forms and symbols so reminiscent of Indian art, Wiley tried to touch upon aspects of American culture unrelated to European-inspired art. He was attempting to establish a set of references with universal application—hence, his delight in constantly finding new meanings for the few symbols he uses regularly. In this anthropological approach, Wiley was moving into a quasi-historical area that many young artists find rewarding today. Wiley's primitivistic constructions are always somehow homespun. There is no sense of academic research. His symbols, carved in wood, burned onto chamois hide, daubed on canvas, gain power through Wiley's repeated use of them. Much of their force comes from the multiple meanings he has imbued them with.

More of a high altar than a totem is the elaborate, rough-edged construction, *Thank You Hide*. As he describes its fabrication, we have some insight into his stream of consciousness approach that brings disparate objects together with unexpected leaps of imagination:

I found the hide at a flea market... brought it home and tacked it on the wall. When it was hanging there, I saw the United States echoed in the shape. I was reading Nietzsche's *Beyond Good and Evil*... I can't remember what it was I read, but it was like these Zen things. I saw something on that hide. "Thank you," I thought. The rest was built up from little objects around the studio... There's a fish lure I found on the beach... some bones... a fishing pole... I figured I was probably fresh bait for Nietzsche.

It Remains to be Seen 1974
construction of branches, tree roots, acrylic on chamois hide, ink and acrylic on wood, metal, string, leather, glass, English walnuts and spray can
51 x 36 x 55
Collection Matthew and Wanda Ashe
Sausalito, California

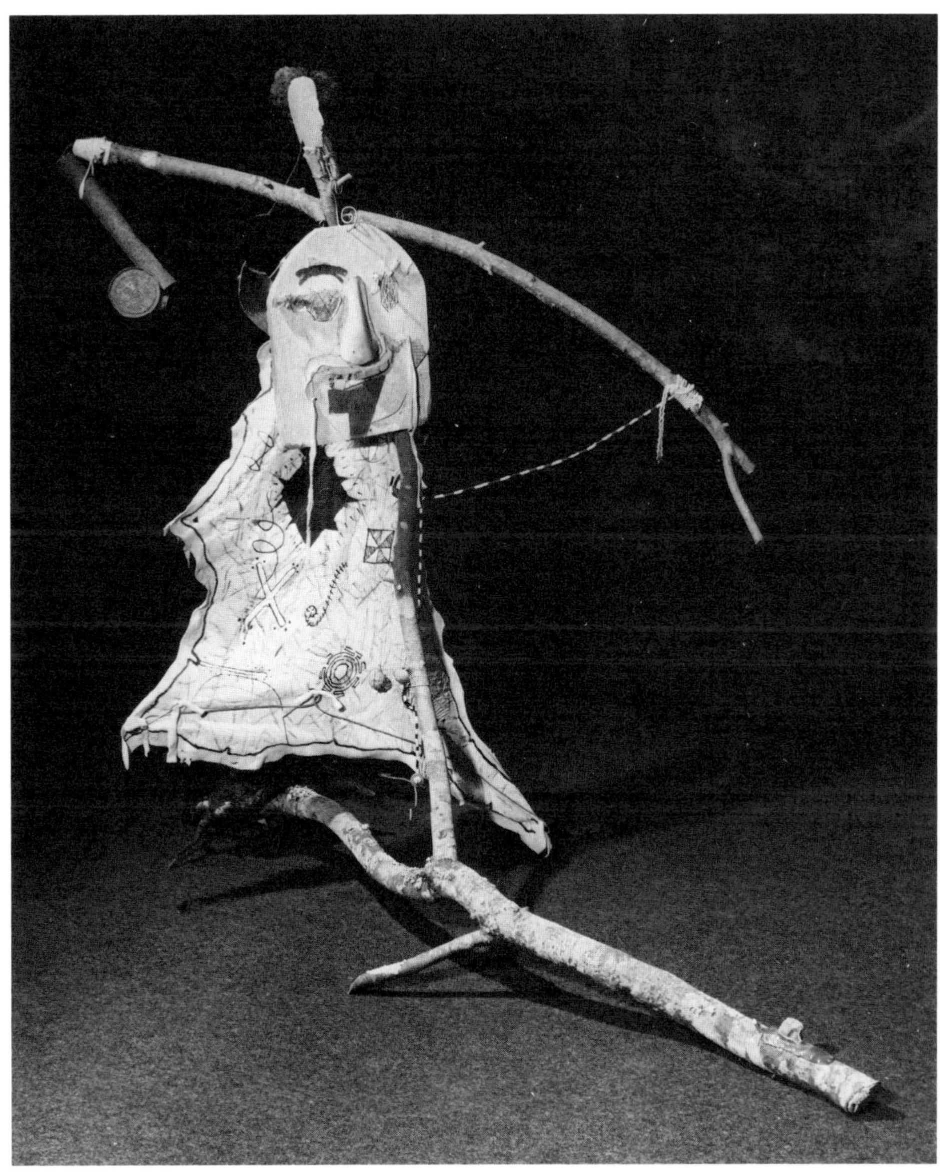

Down the Line with Ol' Sir Rot 1975
construction of wood, branch, metal, leather
and found objects
33 x 13½ x 11
drawing of watercolor and ink on paper
30 x 22
Collection Ralph H. Perkins and Steven Smith
Chicago

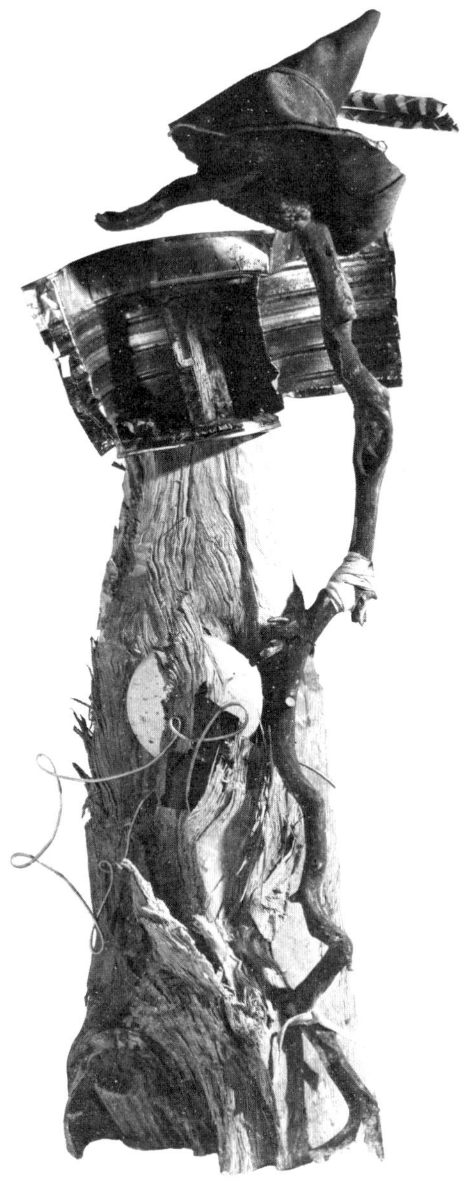

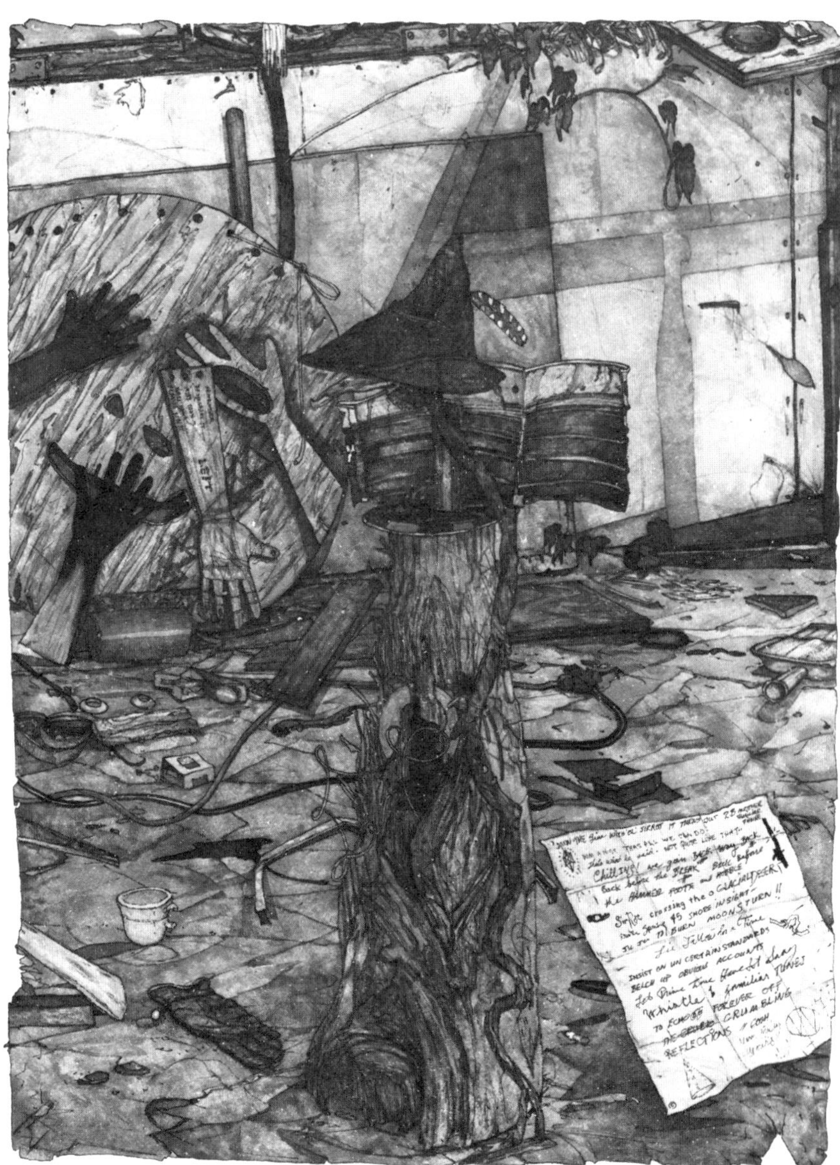

Down The Line with Ol' Sir Rot

In a curious inversion of the usual working process, Wiley frequently bases his small watercolor drawings on his three-dimensional constructions, and the two elements are often exhibited as one work. Drawings of his constructions vary from the fairly straightforward rendition of *Wizdumb Bridge*, to the elaborate spatial and textural treatment of *Down the Line with Ol' Sir Rot*, 1975. Wiley drew the construction *Sir Rot* as it stood in the familiar surroundings of his back yard. In the watercolor, surrounded by other works of art propped up at odd angles, the construction becomes a jaunty scarecrow figure in a landscape of compatible forms. Sir Rot is as much at home in his rag-tag world as de Chirico's brooding, faceless mannequins are in their austere landscapes. The fearsome head of *The Bite Despite*, a 1975 construction, combines a jaw bone and a manzanita root. As this work lay in the studio, Wiley was struck by the way that certain shapes on the floor—cracks, spills and other stains—echoed the shapes of his ferocious creation. Consequently, in the watercolor that now accompanies the construction, the head dominates one of Wiley's abstract landscapes and is shown with a pair of dice and a paint brush, symbolizing the essential ingredients of Wiley's art: the adventurer's luck and the painter's skill.

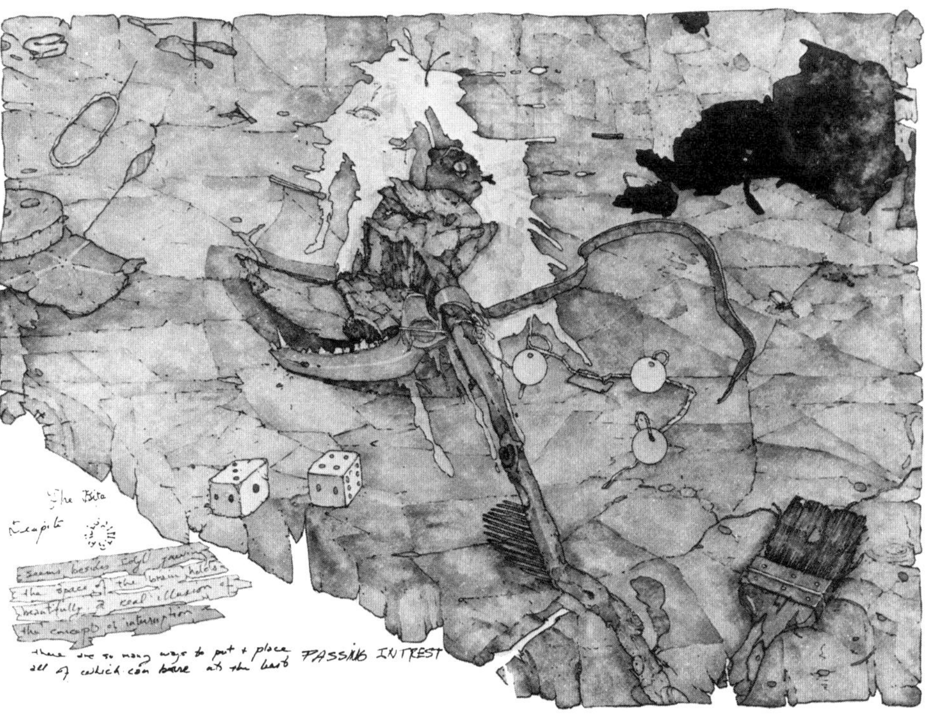

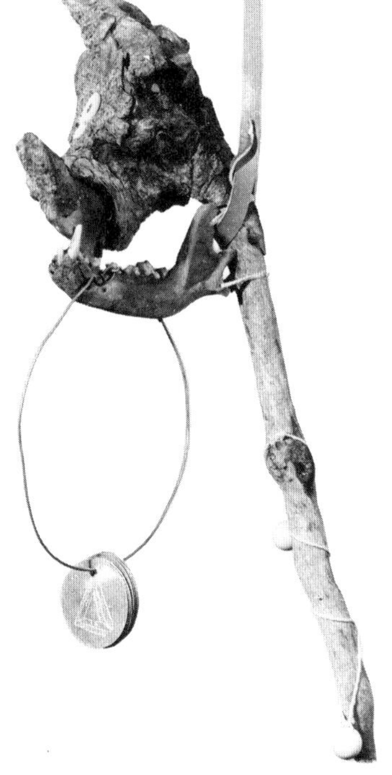

The Bite Despite 1975
construction of branch, bone, leather, metal
and found objects
58 x 12 x 14
drawing of watercolor and ink on paper
22 x 30
Collection Sarah Estribou
Carmel, California

Mr. Unatural and Friends

Wiley, as is often observed, has a striking appearance. Tall and lean, with chiseled features and a large moustache, he resembles a frontier sheriff (the real article of the daguerreotypes, not a John Wayne or James Arness). This impression is further strengthened by his deep voice and slow speech that lend authority to his quiet utterences. Though capable of hilarious antics and quick to laugh, his demeanor is essentially one of poise and dignity.

Wiley's lean physique and long dark hair make him easy to recognize when he depicts himself in his work. Occasionally, as in *What's More in French*, 1977, he appears as himself—the artist. Usually, though, he adopts alter egos. Metaphors for his psyche, particularly its meditative, foolish and capricious aspects, these surrogate figures allow him to make forceful, sometimes illogical, associations precluded by a more straightforwardly autobiographical approach.

One of the earliest personae is Zenry. "He's a combination of Zen and Henry, a little character from the funny papers when I was a kid. He had one curly hair sticking up, a little pointed nose and no mouth. He was mute, never said a thing. He was a little figure that interacted with various situations and scenes, but could only express himself with marks."

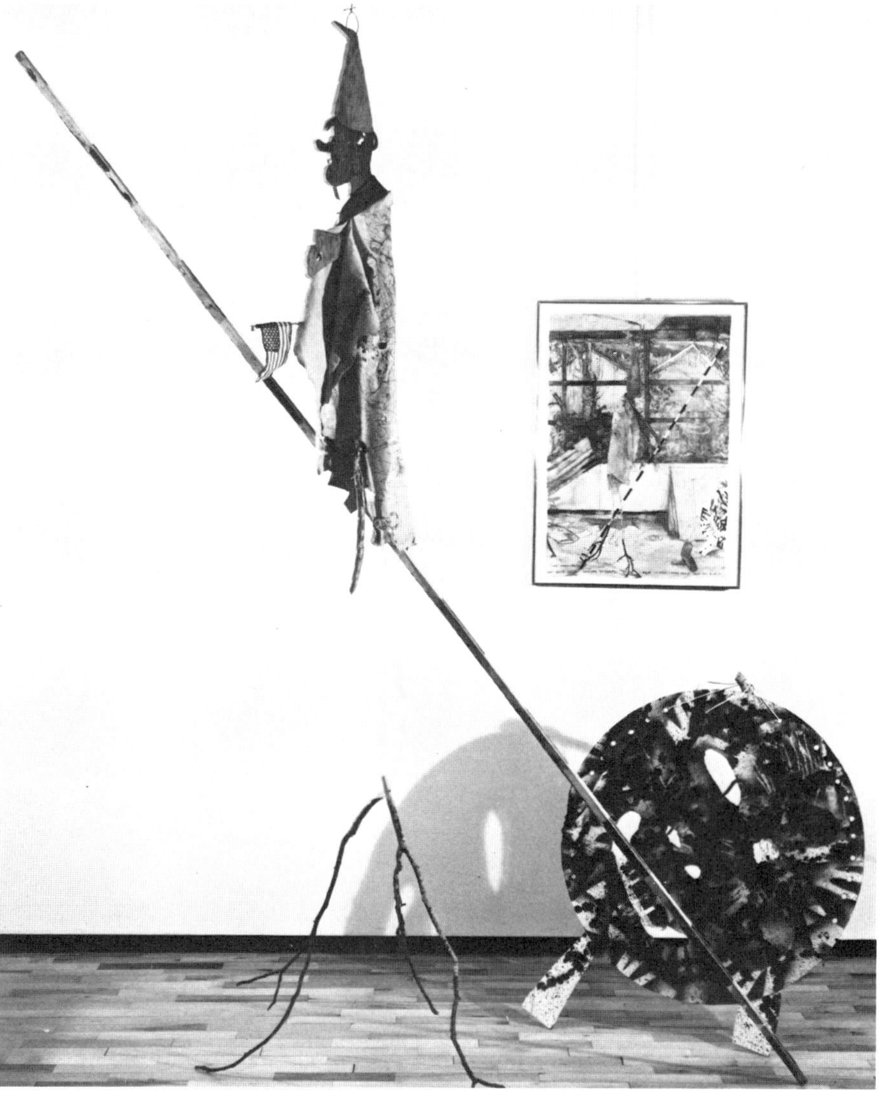

Mr. Unatural and Friends 1976
two-part construction of watercolor, colored pencil and lithography on chamois hide, plywood, rubber, cloth, wood, enamel and beans
38 x 30 x 29; 91 x 82 x 21
drawing of watercolor and ink on paper
31 x 23
Collection Mr. and Mrs. Gerald W. Bush
Sewickley, Pennsylvania

Zenry 1974
construction of tree stump, ink on wood, manzanita, wood, rope, wire, glass and bones
36 x 38 x 15
Courtesy Delahunty Gallery
Dallas

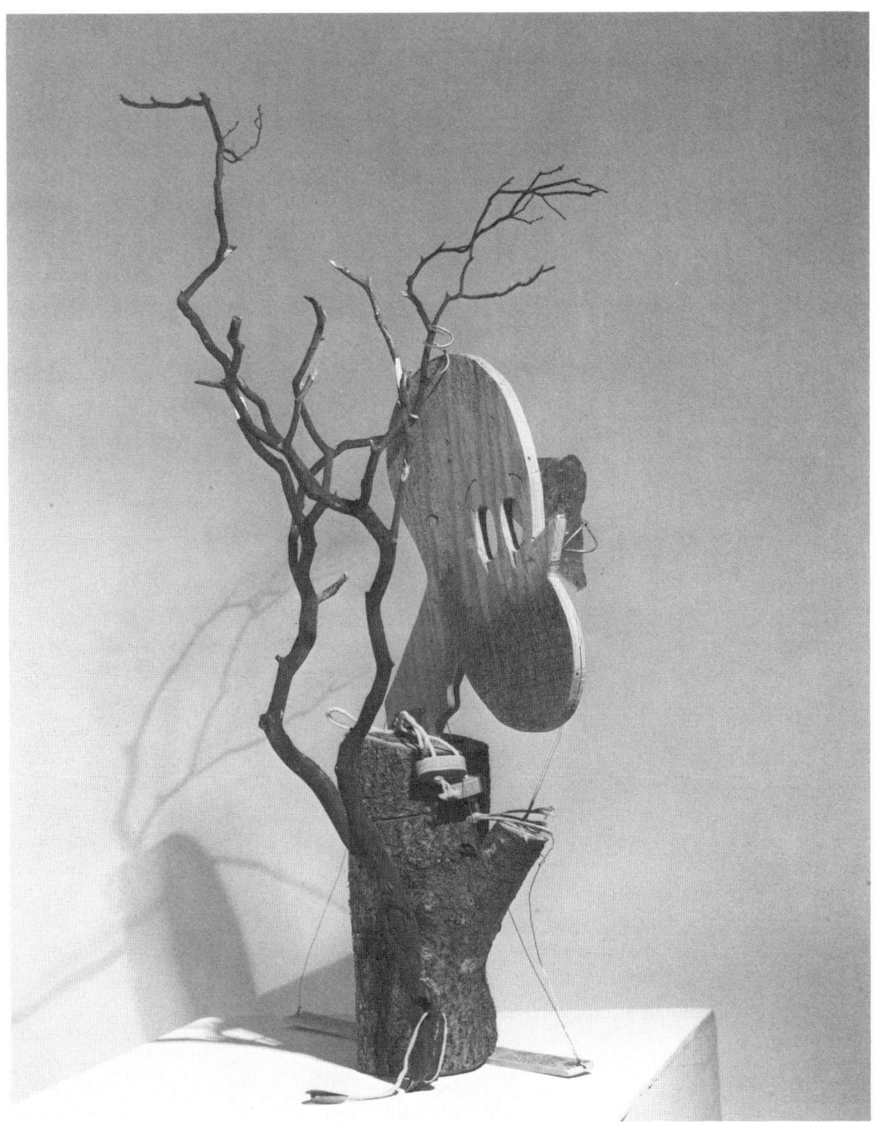

In the construction, *Zenry,* 1974, the cutout, wood silhouette of Zenry's head sits on a log. The manzanita branch adorning his head is, Wiley says, "lightning striking—Enlightenment." Zenry, then, who appears as a vulnerable figure in the nightmarish drawing, *Lord Half Mercy,* 1975, and as the inspiring force in *What's Left of the Garden and Mirror,* is Wiley, quietly meandering through life, making his own associations and observations.

The characters, Rim Rat, Ray Done and Sir Rot, are references to artists (Rembrandt, Redon, Seurat, respectively) and were inspired by Wiley's sudden interest in "dark drawings" when working on the Landfall Press book, *Suite of Daze.* The lanky, Wiley-like silhouette, Mr. Nobody, of the 1973 painting, was partly an homage to Alberto Giacometti, though transformed into a Zen-inspired void.

By far the most persistent of Wiley's personae is the wise-fool, Mr. Unatural, a scrawny, gangling figure with a large, fake nose, dressed in a black kimono, conical hat and high Japanese clogs. Several critics have somehow seen this self-portrait as inspired by Robert Crumb's short, fat, bearded guru, Mr. Natural, but, as is usually the case with Wiley, this symbolic character grew out of the stuff of his daily life.

Wiley once made a rough sketch of a figure symbolizing occasions when, he felt, he had made a fool of himself. He called the figure Mr. Unatural. This character came into focus when Dan Snyder, a friend who teaches theater at the University of California, Davis, asked Wiley to participate in an annual improvisational performance, *Out our Way.* Doubting his skills as an actor, Wiley felt he "needed some sort of cover and thought of Mr. Unatural." Then, if the logic of any action was questioned, Wiley could respond, "Well, what could be more unnatural."

Mr. Unatural's outfit incorporates symbols from the paintings—he bears them like the attributes of a saint from an Italian altar piece. The range pole is his staff, the triangle form becomes a pointed cap. The writing on the cap proclaims Mr. Unatural to be a dunce, but the cabalistic signs written there also suggest he is a wizard. In the performances, words and symbols can be written on the child's blackboard Mr. Unatural wears around his neck for, like Zenry, Mr. Unatural does not speak.

Nothing Conforms 1978
watercolor and ink on paper
30 x 22
Collection Whitney Museum of American Art
New York

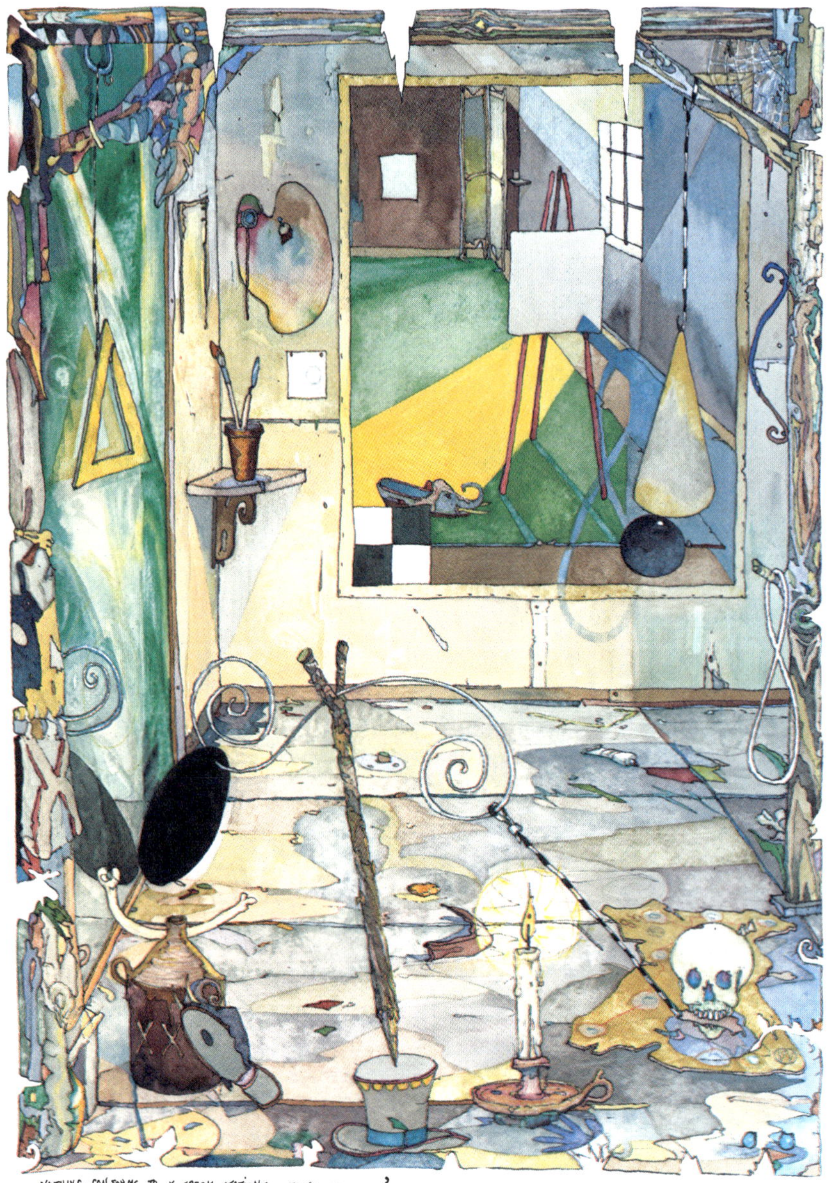

Ultimately, behind all the metaphors, the autobiography, the jokes and off-hand gestures, Wiley's art revolves around the concept of metamorphosis. The essence of his pun—the verbal trickery of the narratives and the visual coincidences of the constructions—is metamorphosis. The ever developing alter ego characters, the elementary symbols that subtly grow as new meanings accrue, the equivocal map and landscape forms—all these are manifestations of interrelationships and change, and the shifting area, where an entity is always on the verge of becoming something else, is Wiley's domain.

Though much of his work seems to rely on paradox, such a notion has no real place in Wiley's universe. As Zen Buddhism teaches, all apparent opposites are reconciled when viewed as part of a continuous chain. The grave and the humorous, the foolish and the wise, the mundane and the mystical are not things to be separated out and reserved for special places or particular times. Without one, the other could not exist.

An eerie mood prevails in recent watercolors. The warm, backwoods freshness of *Lame and Blind in Eden* has been replaced by the brittle, crystalline colors that transpose Wiley's familiar, friendly studio into the fugitive spaces of *Nothing Conforms*, 1978. Wiley acknowledges the recent shift in emphasis. It is, he asserts, simply the other side of the same coin.

> I'd have to say, some of it is getting older, seeing death is closer. There's nothing that makes you feel more alive than contemplating death. Plus, it's something in this society we're absolutely terrified of... People see it only as negative image, don't see any positive aspects of it in terms of actually confronting one's own mortality and space you're presently occupying... I have to bring that reference in there and not be afraid to look at it... I know the negative aspect is there, but there's no way to separate the two.

Thus, Wiley welcomes everything as having potential for his art. He believes that lessons are to be learned from the most unexpected sources. Wiley's art deals with the limitless possibilities of the human mind.

Twelve years ago he finally learned that what counts in creating a work of art is not regard—or disregard—for a set of formal rules, but an integrity of approach that respects all things as having artistic potential. Wiley's all inclusive approach—reflected in the astonishing range of his imagery and materials—disconcerts some critics who see it as a basic inability to be selective. It is true that an open minded stance can easily lapse into an unquestioning one, but Wiley is more selective than he seems at first sight. Out of the abundant images that enrich his paintings and constructions, a few emerge with central importance. An allegorist of the first order, Wiley has evolved a potent, versatile iconography. By persistent use, he has invested a handful of motifs with symbolic power, transporting them from the specific circumstances of his life in Marin County to a poetic realm.

Paintings

Bob's Hide 1971
acrylic on felt with rope, paper, plastic and wood
90 x 72
Collection Elaine Horwitch
Phoenix, Arizona

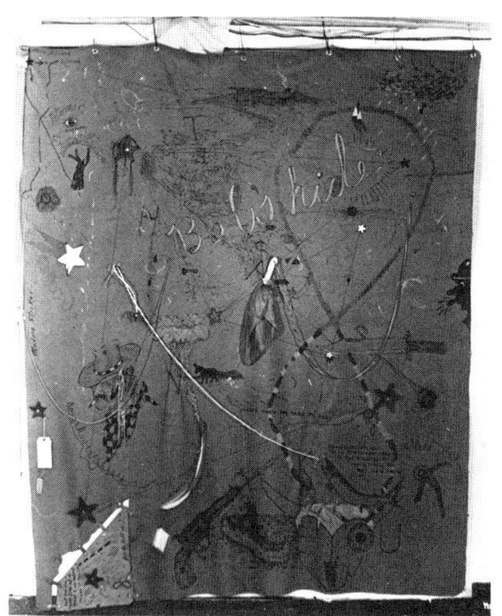

Nothing Personal 1972
acrylic on canvas
42½ x 42½
Collection Maxine and Jerry Silberman
Glencoe, Illinois

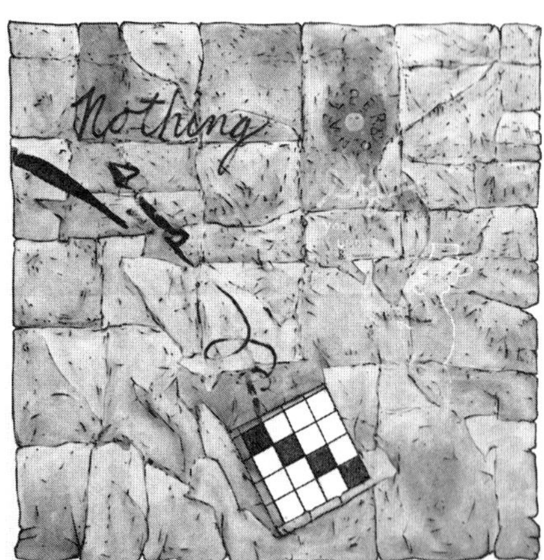

Not Exactly Straight 1973
acrylic, charcoal and ink on canvas
54 x 113
Collection Byron R. Meyer
San Francisco

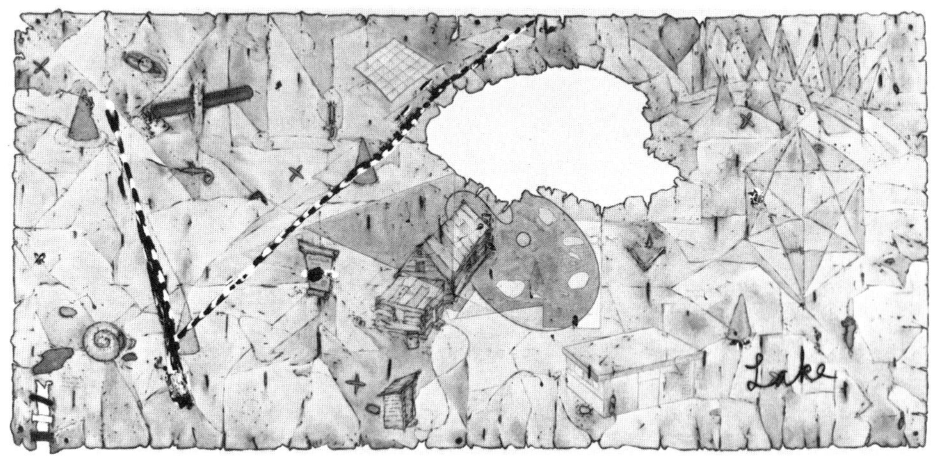

I Won't Forget Again One Jillion Times 1973
acrylic, charcoal and ink on canvas
96 x 156
Collection Walker Art Center, Minneapolis
Purchased with matching grant from Museum
Purchase Plan, National Endowment
for the Arts

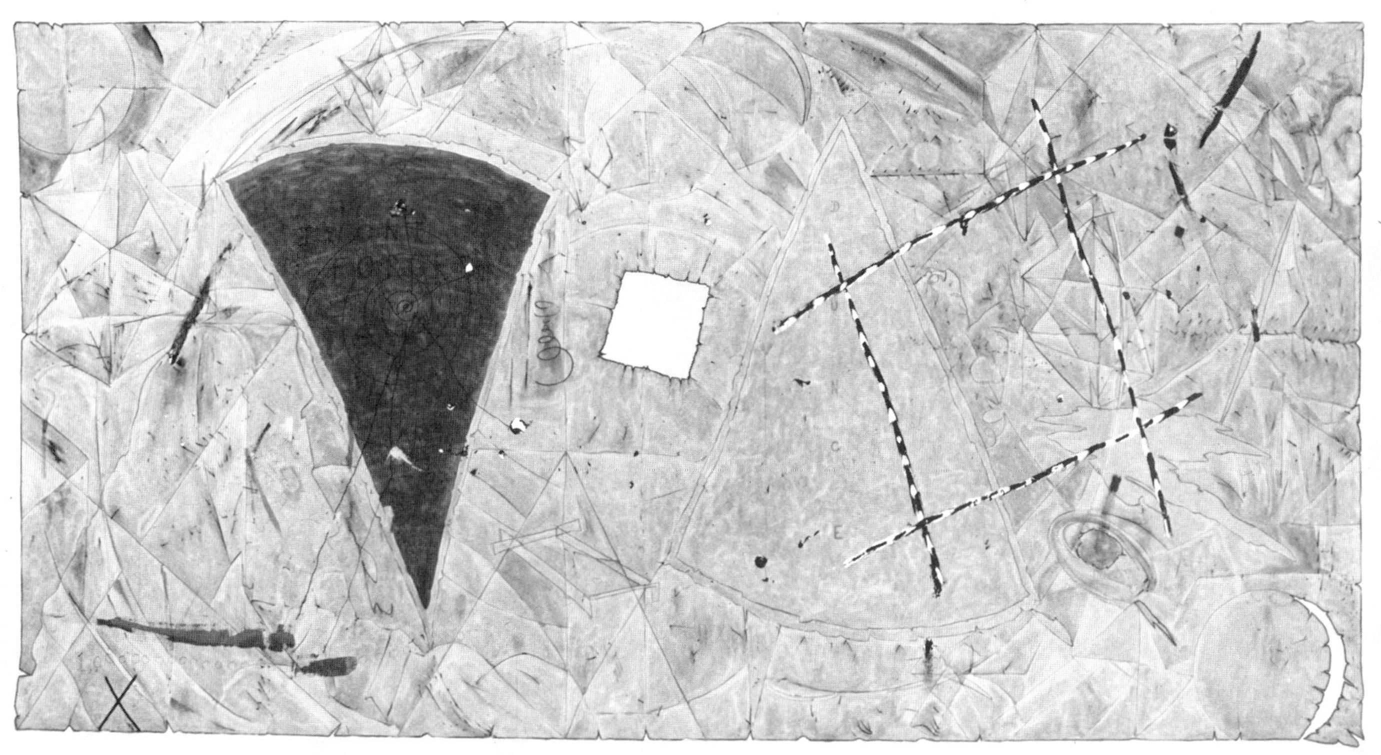

Village Green 1974
acrylic and charcoal on canvas
88½ x 77½
Collection Robert A. Rowan
Pasadena, California

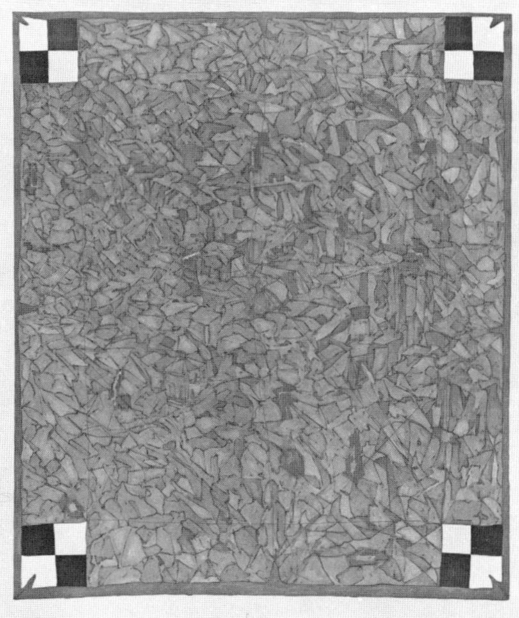

Quivering on the Path 1974
painting of acrylic on canvas
90 x 180
construction of wood, branch, Plexiglas, wire, quartz cry'stal, metal and found objects
68 x 32 x 118
Collection Fort Worth Art Museum
Purchased by the Benjamin J. Tillar Memorial Trust Fund

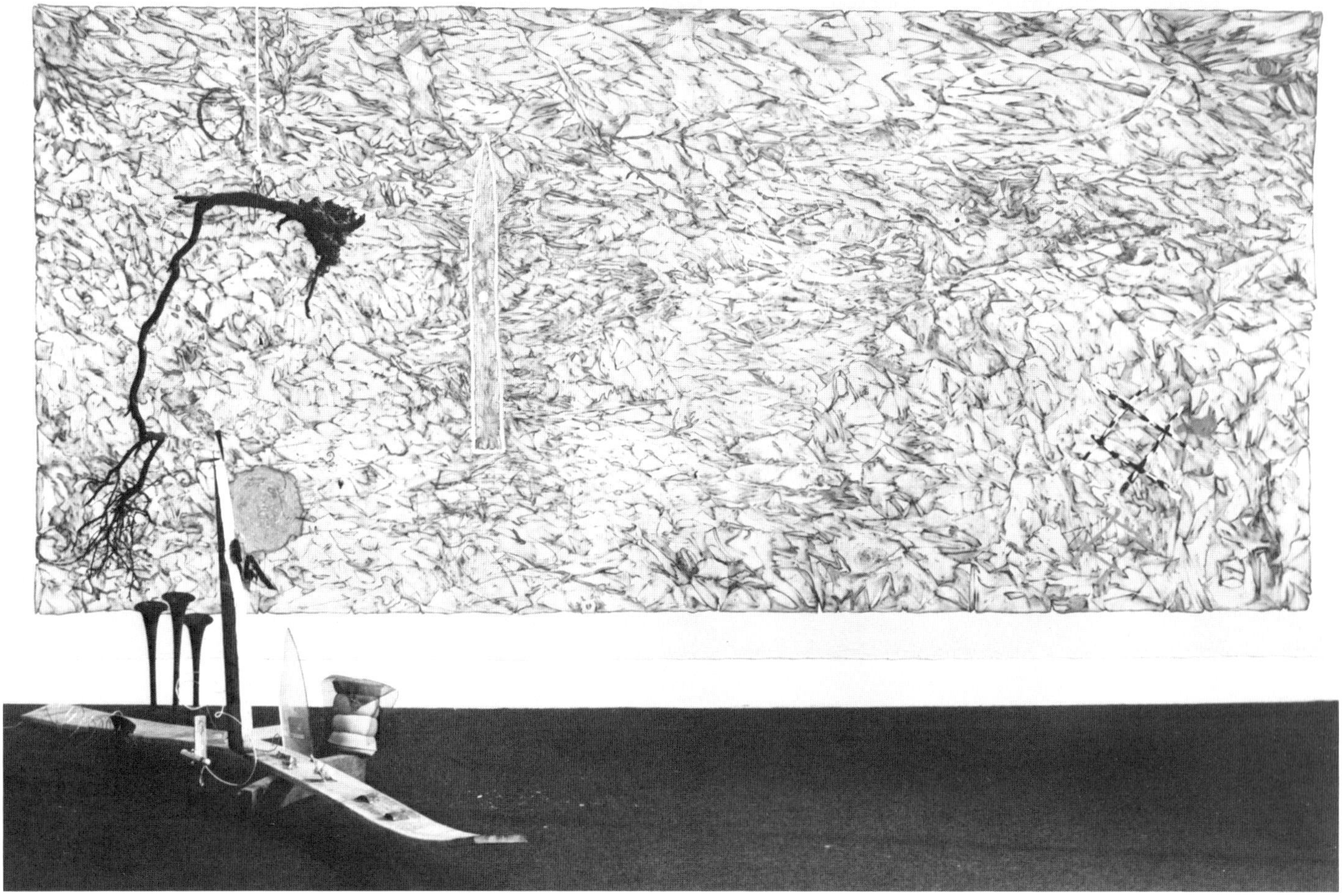

The Nature of the Beast 1975
acrylic and charcoal on canvas
100½ x 97
Collection The Baltimore Museum of Art
Museum Purchase: W. Clagett Emory Bequest Fund

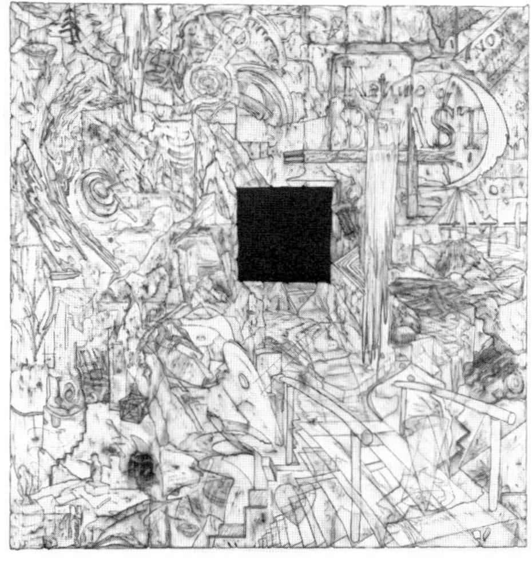

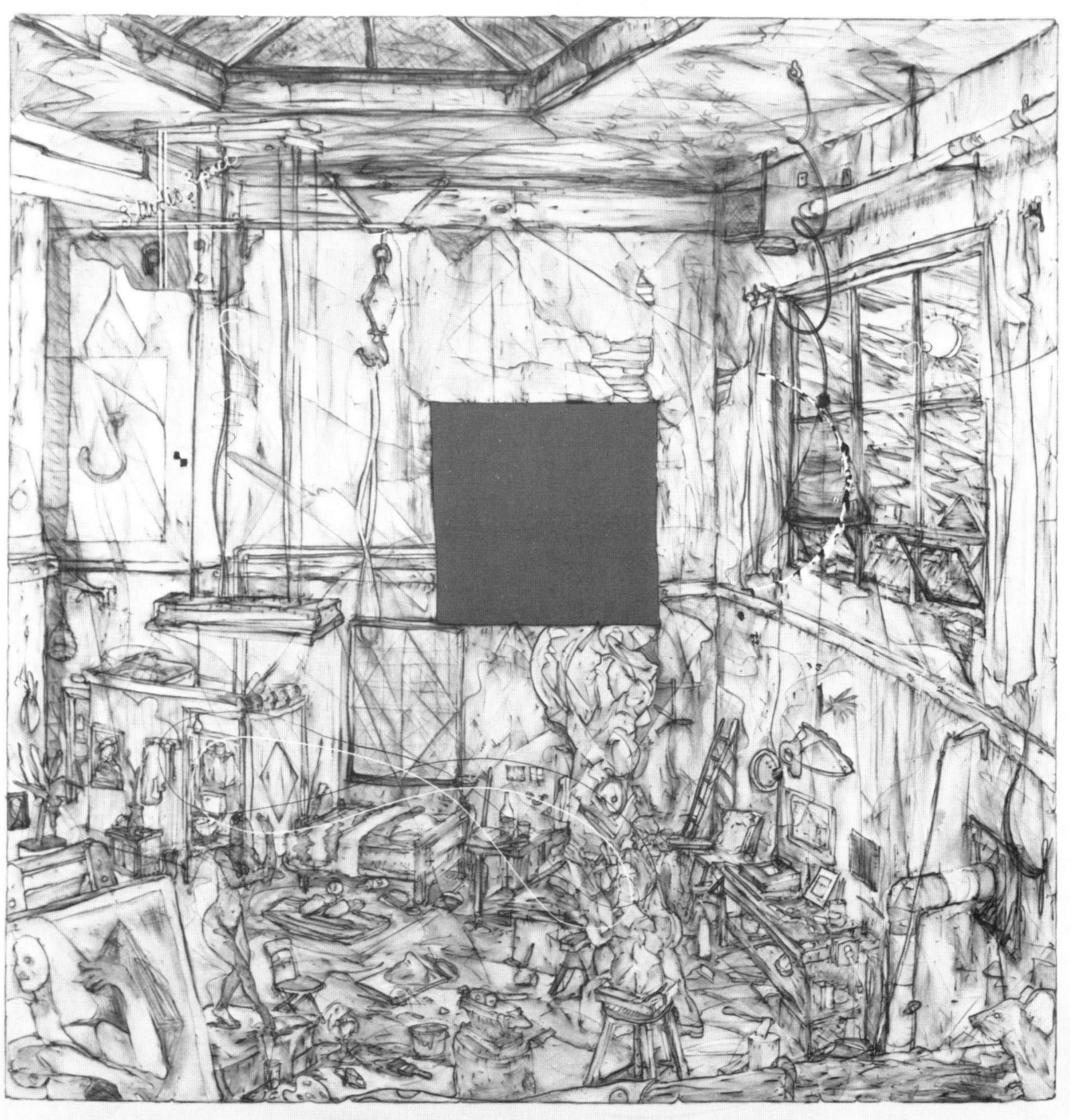

Studio Space 1975
acrylic and charcoal on canvas
83 x 80¾
Collection Robert A. Rowan
Pasadena, California

Hot Jazz Pntng. with No Music 1976
acrylic and charcoal on canvas
72 x 96
Collection Diana Fuller
San Francisco

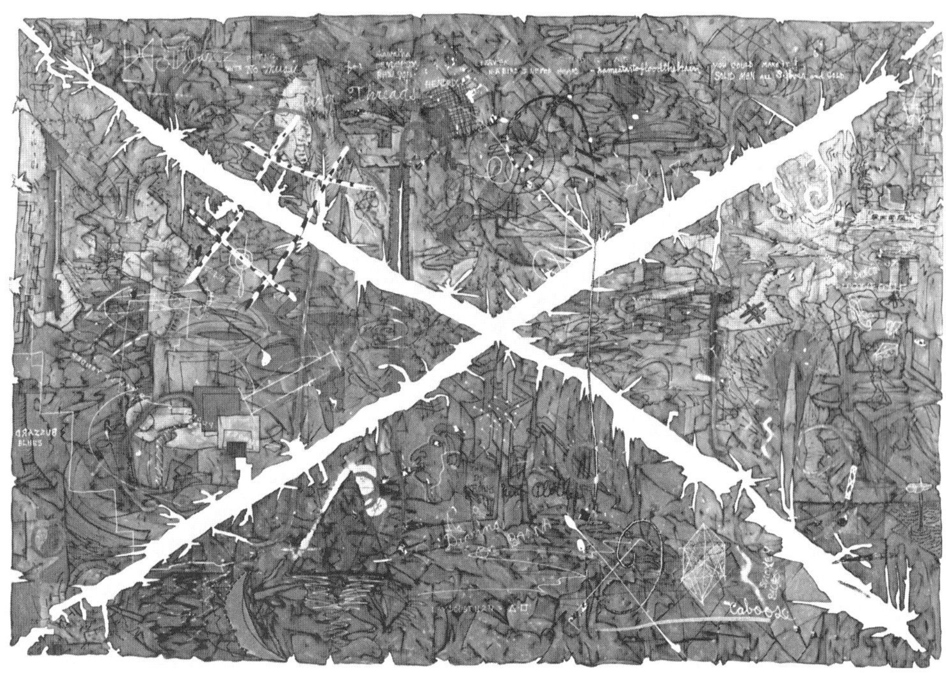

Ol Uncle Sam with Sword 1976
painting of acrylic and pastel on canvas
97 x 63¼ x 14½ (irregular)
construction of ink on wood, wire and leather
Collection William H. Plummer
Chicago

Self Portrait #1 1977
acrylic on paper
20 x 14
Private Collection

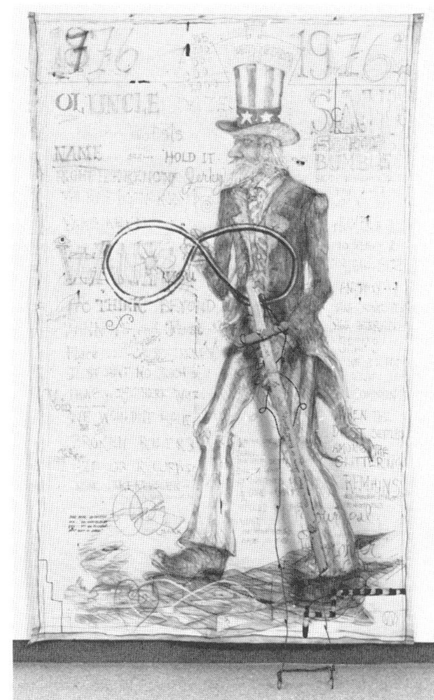

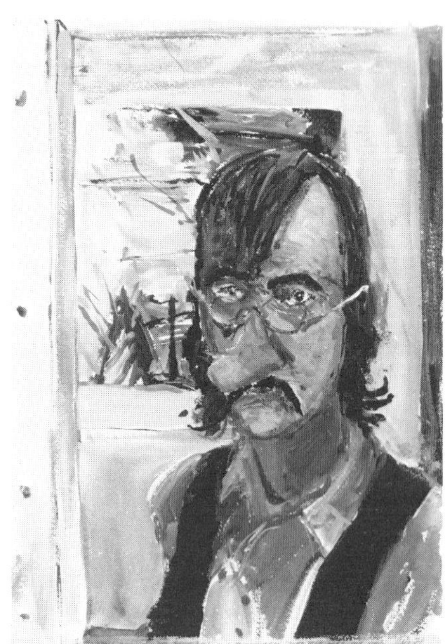

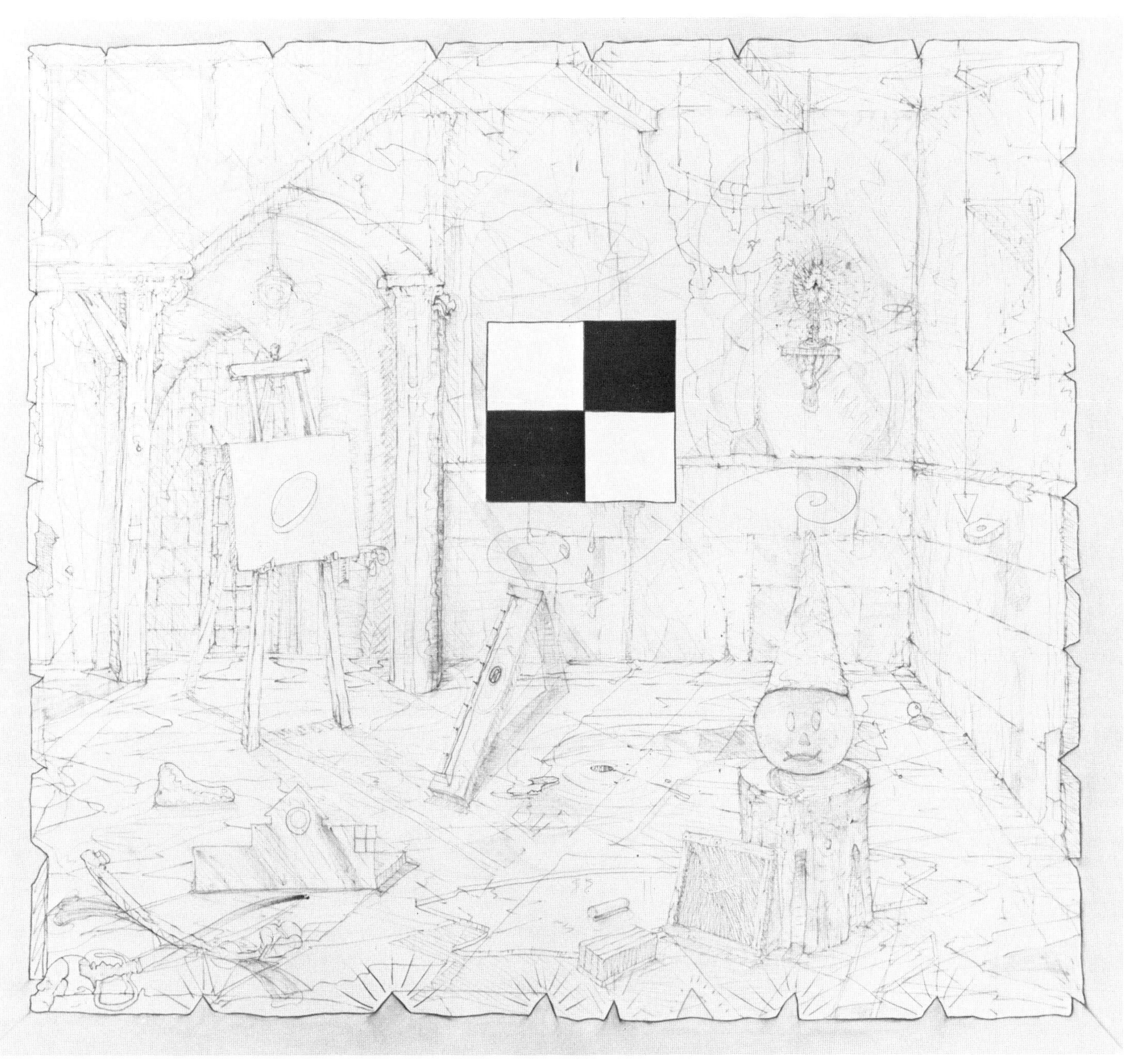

Nothing Changes 1977
acrylic, charcoal and pastel on canvas
80 x 89⅜
Collection Richard and Roseylne Swig
San Francisco

M.C.T.O.T./Getting the Drift of It 1978
painting of acrylic and charcoal on canvas
89 x 89
drawing of colored pencil, charcoal and wax
on parchment
36 x 24¾
Collection Mr. and Mrs. William Wilson III
Hillsborough, California

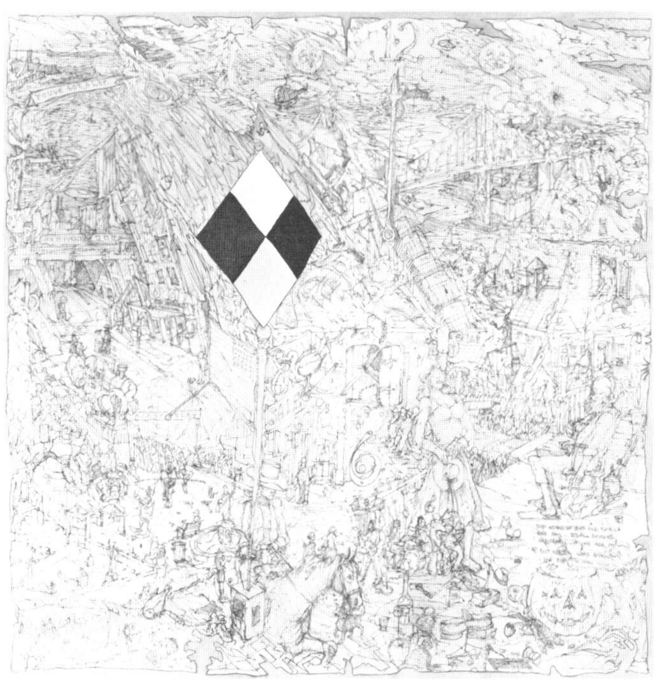

All Saints Ball 1978
acrylic and charcoal on canvas
30 x 30
Collection Stephen Alpert
Wayland, Massachusetts

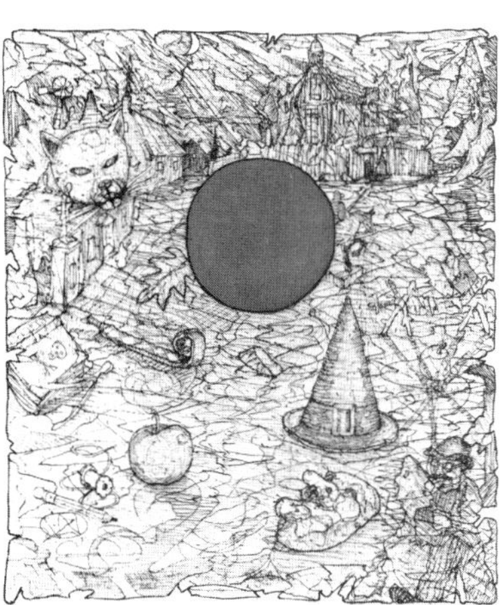

O.T.P.A.G. 1978
acrylic and graphite on canvas
87¼ x 100¼
Collection Mr. and Mrs. William C. Janss
Sun Valley, Idaho

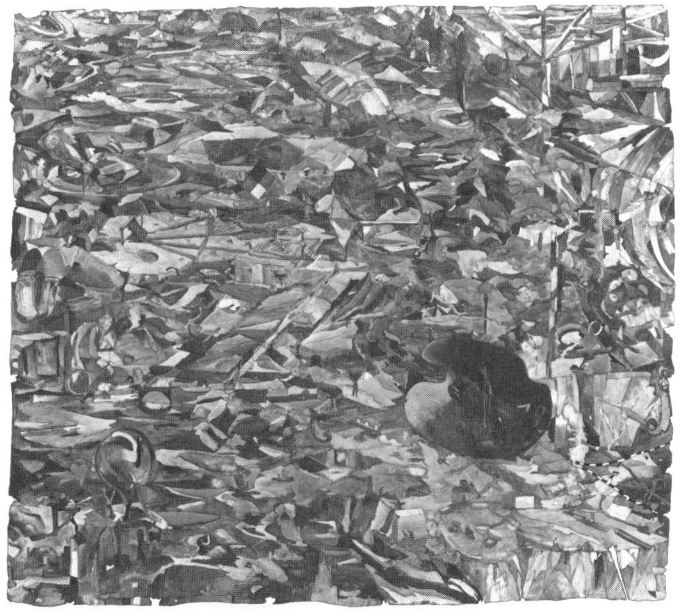

Watercolors and Drawings

How to Fold a Painting 1967
watercolor and ink of buff drawing paper
25½ x 30¾
Private Collection

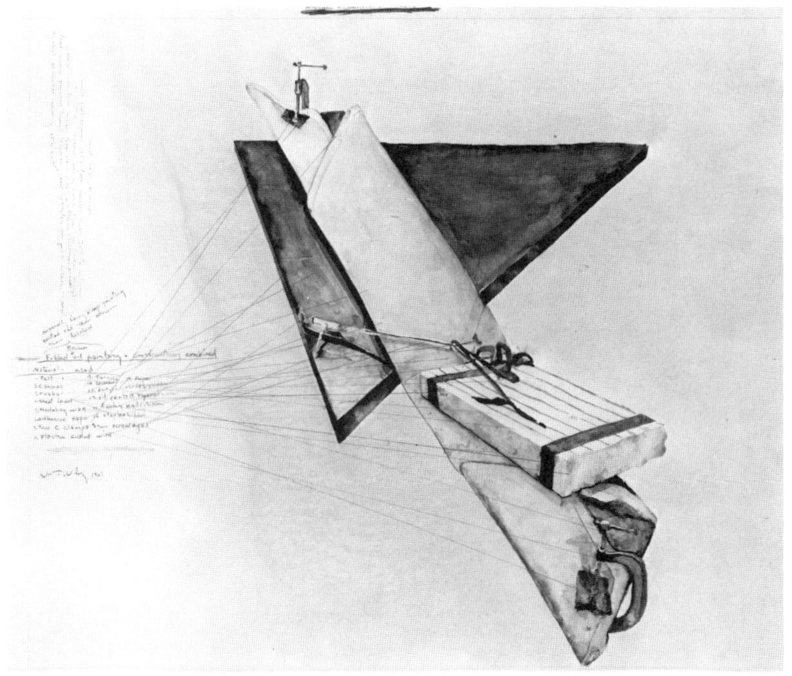

Modern Sculpture with Weakness 1967
watercolor and ink on paper
28½ x 22½
Courtesy Allan Frumkin Gallery
New York

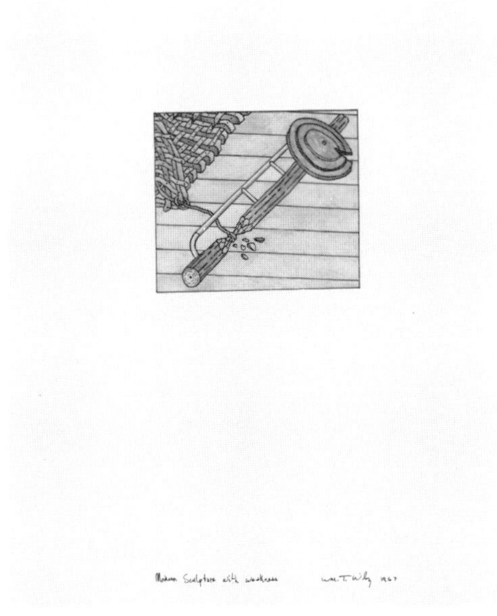

Changing the Whole Time 1969
watercolor and ink on paper
30 x 22
Private Collection

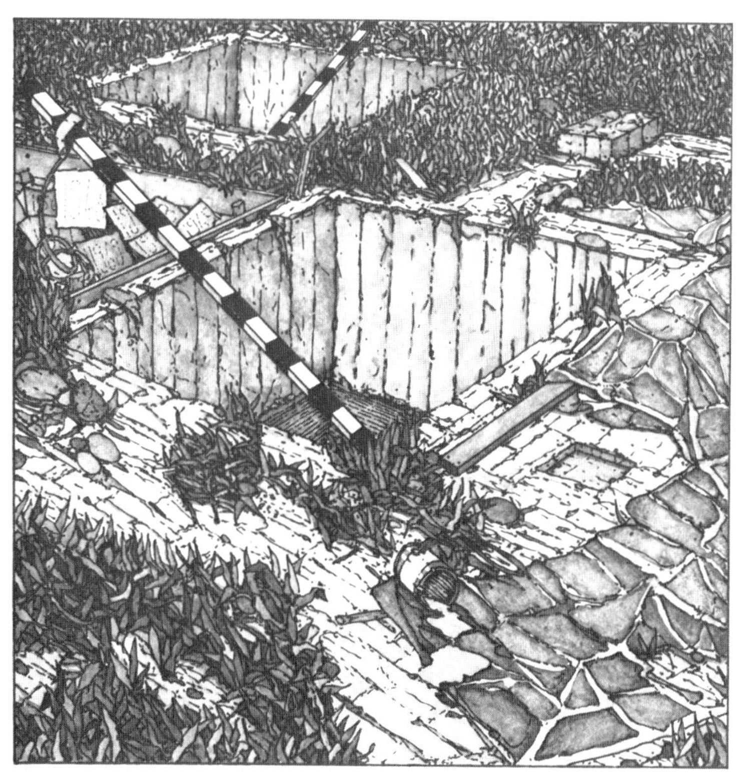

Changing the Whole Timre

Science being the measure of. And the kinds of destruction leveled against the Earth. Exploding huge bombs. Radiating. Various forms of a gas. The real measure will be explored in terms of repair & salvage. And the clear evidence will minimize the most advanced forms of Absurdity.

Wm. T. Wiley 1969

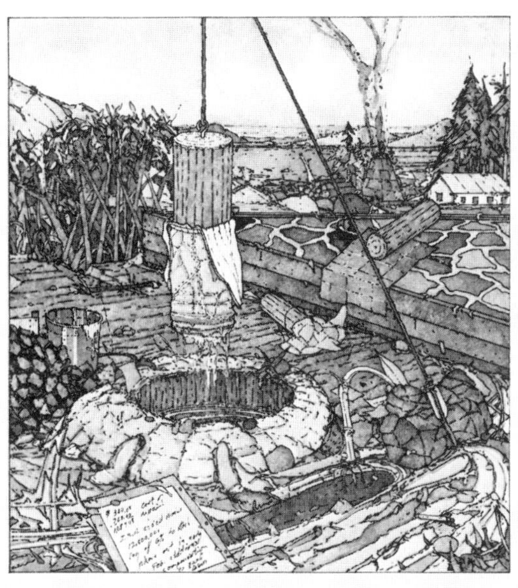

Hung Up Not Far from the Mill 1969
watercolor and ink on paper
30 x 22
Collection Alice Adam
Chicago

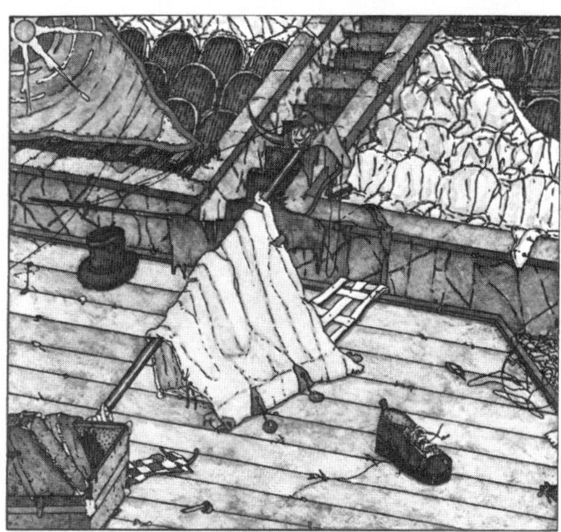

Watching the Poor Play 1969
watercolor and ink on paper
24 x 19
Collection John Garofalos and Mary Gremley
Mill Valley, California

The Balance is Not so Far Away from the Good Old Daze 1970
watercolor and ink on paper
22 x 30
Collection David Lawrence
Chicago

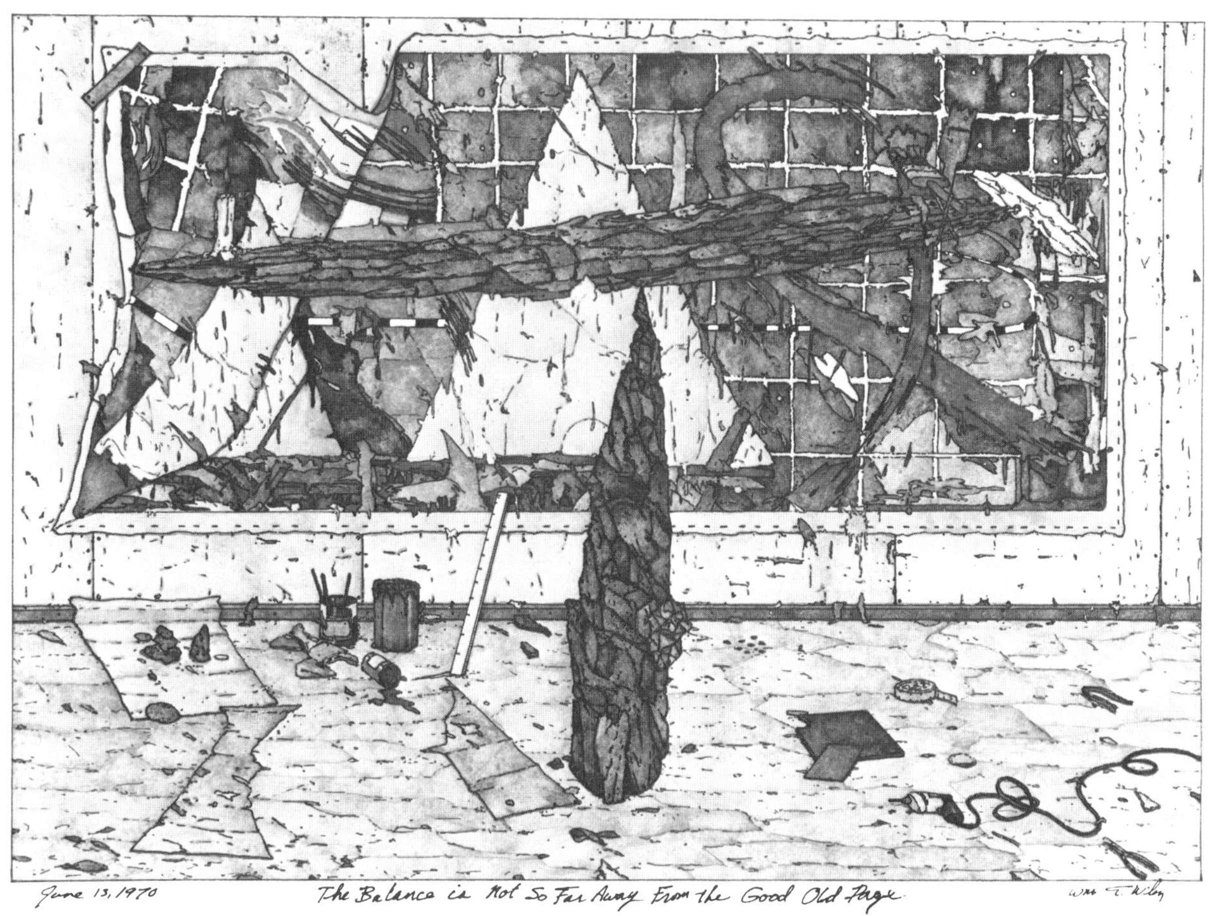

The Years Harvest a Strange Lot Eqaul to None 1969
watercolor and ink on paper
22 x 30
Collection Louis D. Fielder
Atherton, California

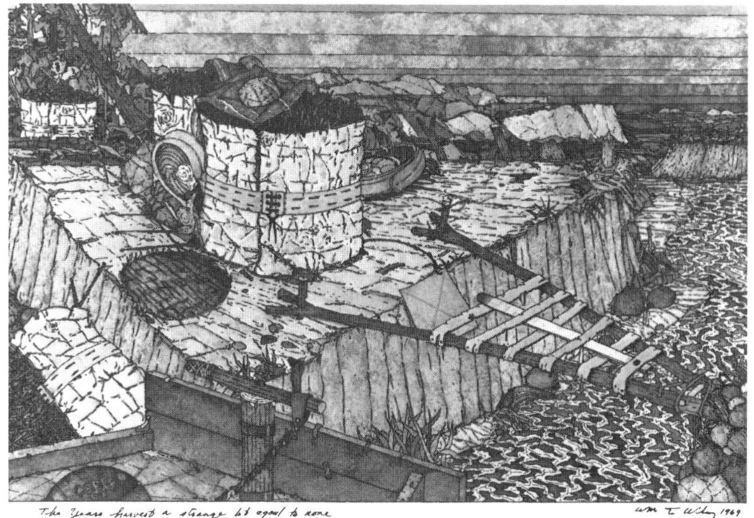

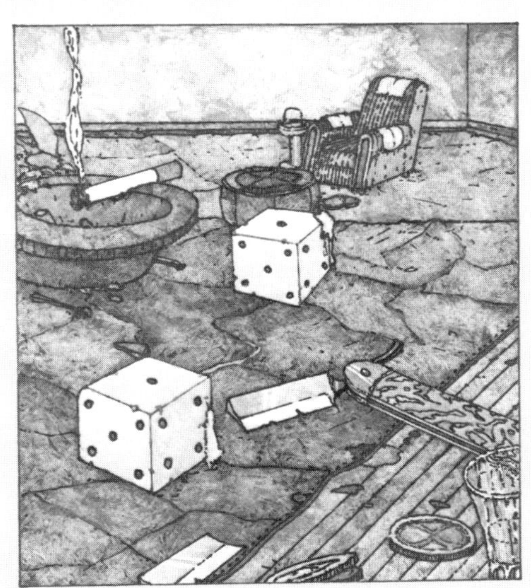

Snake Eyes, Glass Eyes 1970
watercolor and ink on paper
23¾ x 19
Courtesy Odyssia Gallery
New York

Sly Mould Restoration 1972
watercolor and ink on paper
22 x 30
Collection Mr. and Mrs. Harry W. Anderson
Atherton, California

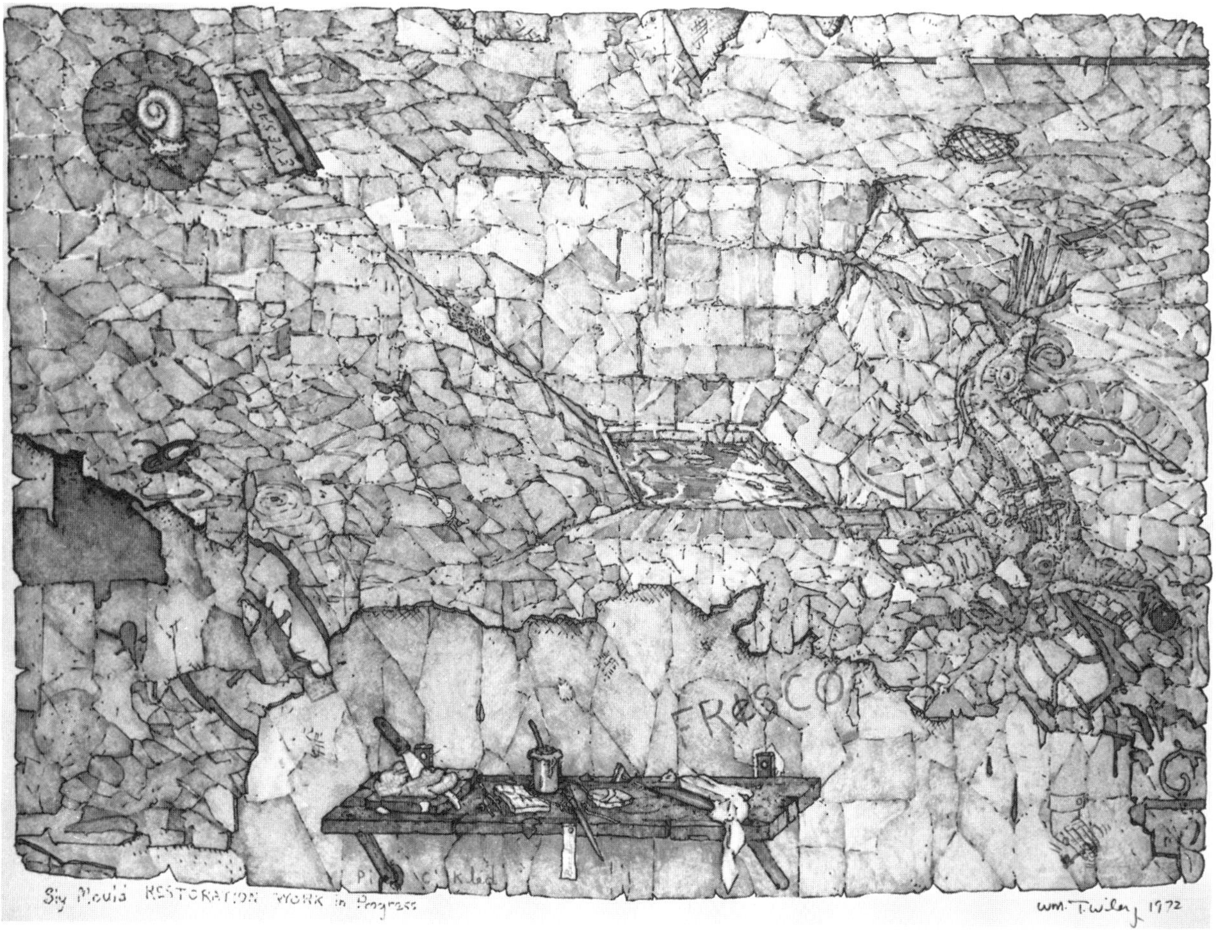

X Stream Art 1970
watercolor and ink on paper
22 x 30
Collection Mr. and Mrs. Lewis Manilow
Chicago

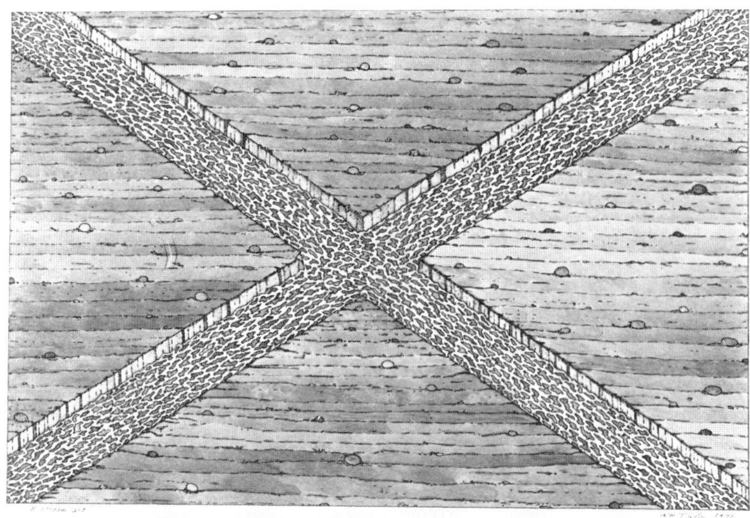

Monday Monster Practice 1972-73
watercolor and ink on paper
18 x 15 (irregular)
Collection Judy and Joseph Raffael
San Geronimo, California

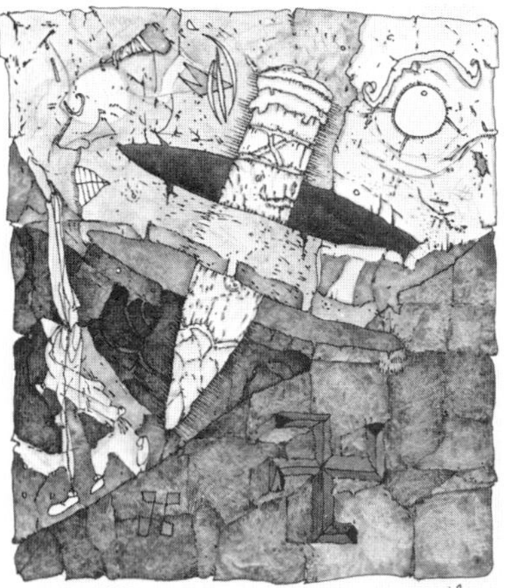

Eye Sword 1973
watercolor, graphite and ink on paper
30 x 22
Collection Mrs. Alexander de Bretteville
San Francisco

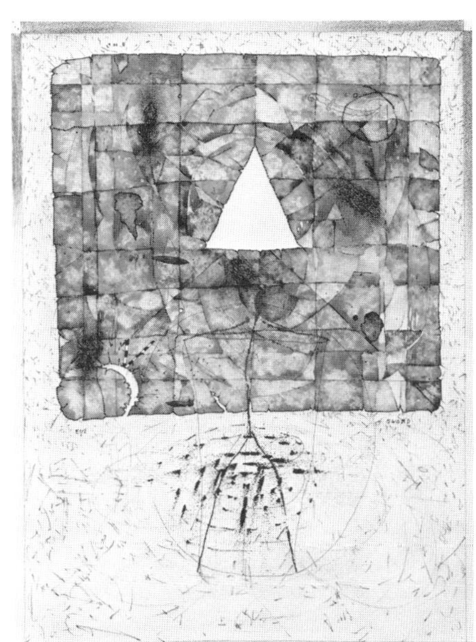

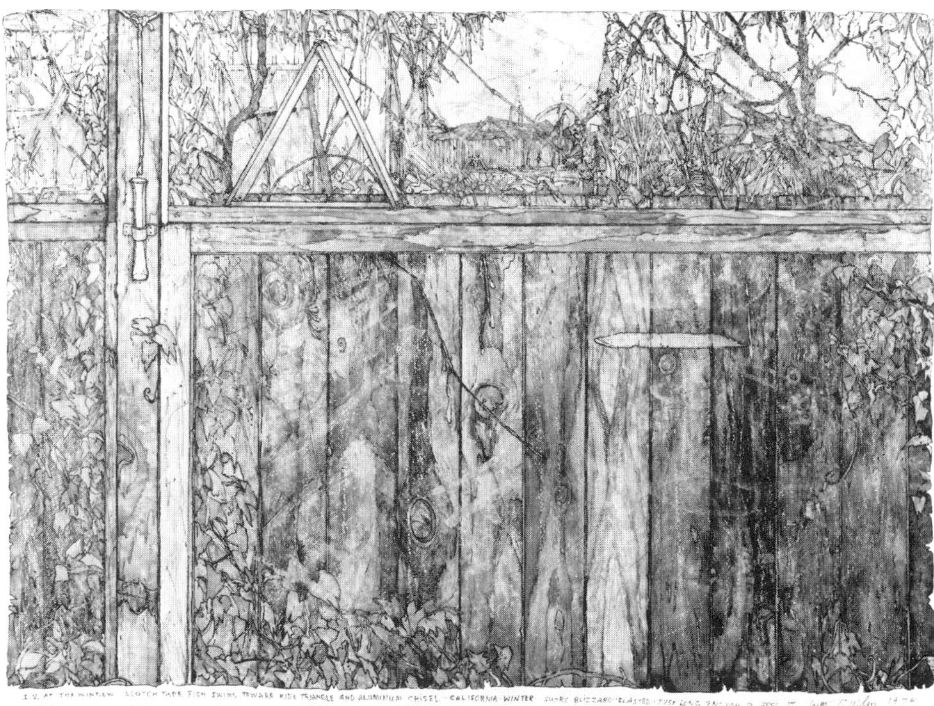

I.V. at the Window 1974
watercolor and ink on paper
22 x 30
Collection Carl E. Horn
Summit, New Jersey

Crude Studease from a Loft 1974
watercolor, ink and graphite on paper
14 x 10
Collection Mr. and Mrs. Leonard S. Meranus
Cincinnati

Natural Drift 1974
watercolor and ink on paper
30 x 22
Courtesy Allan Frumkin Gallery
New York

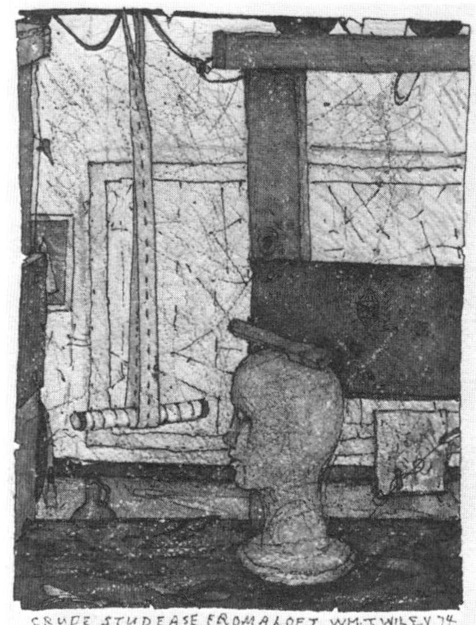

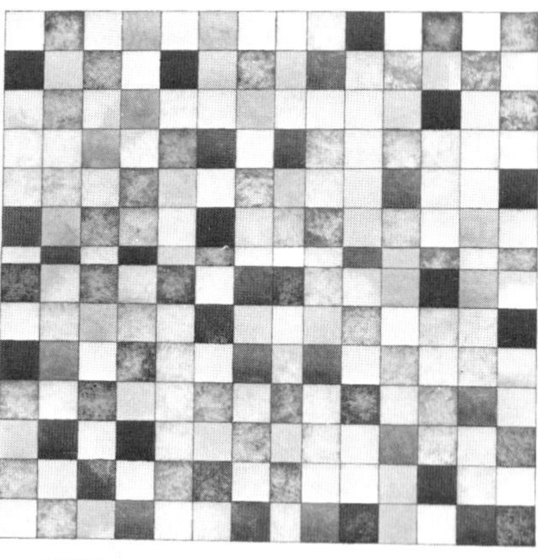

Rim Rats Cabin 1975
watercolor, ink, graphite and colored pencil
on paper
30 x 22
Collection Sarah Estribou
Carmel, California

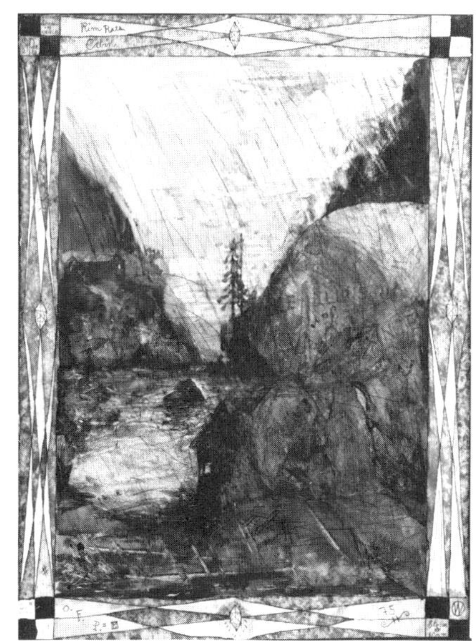

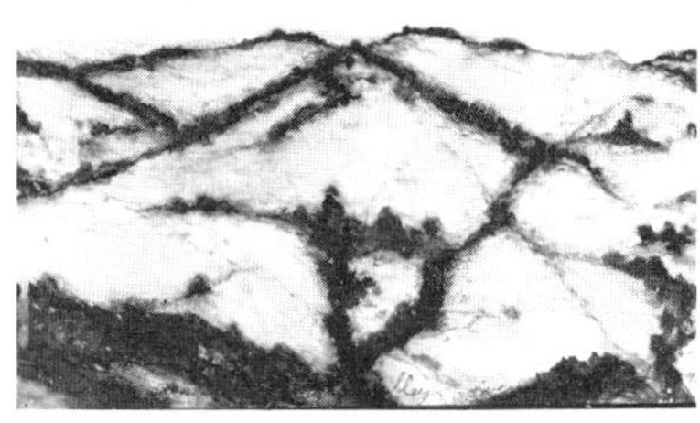

Poon Kinney Ridge 1974
watercolor and ink on paper
10 x 14
Collection Mr. and Mrs. C. David Robinson
Sausalito, California

Night Herding 1975
graphite, charcoal, watercolor and colored pencil on buff drawing paper
36 x 26
Collection Robert A. Rowan
Pasadena, California

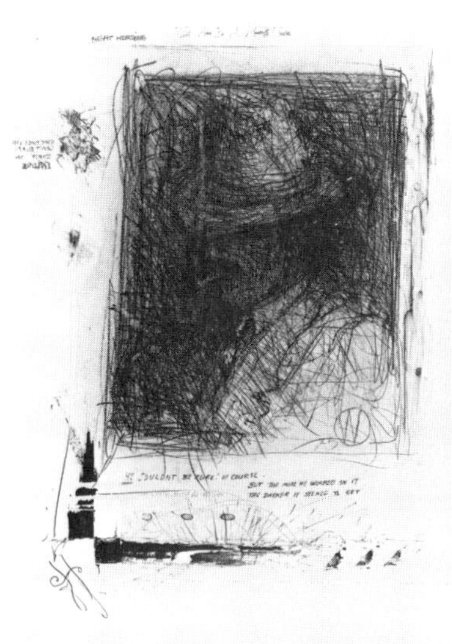

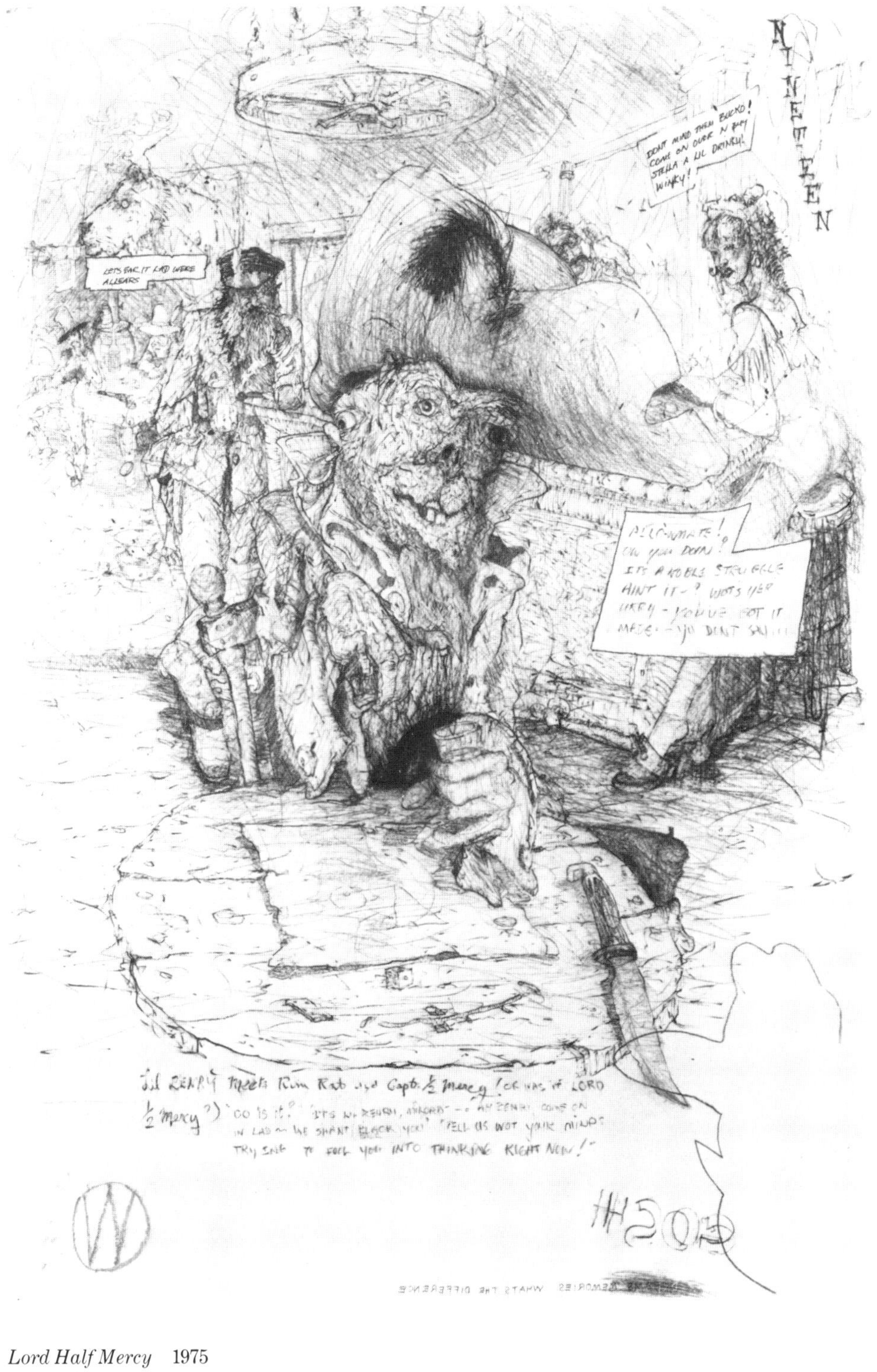

Lord Half Mercy 1975
charcoal on paper
36 x 24½
Collection Mr. and Mrs. E. A. Bergman
Chicago

Pure Chance 1975
watercolor and ink on paper
10 x 14
Collection Jacqueline and Myron Blank
Des Moines, Iowa

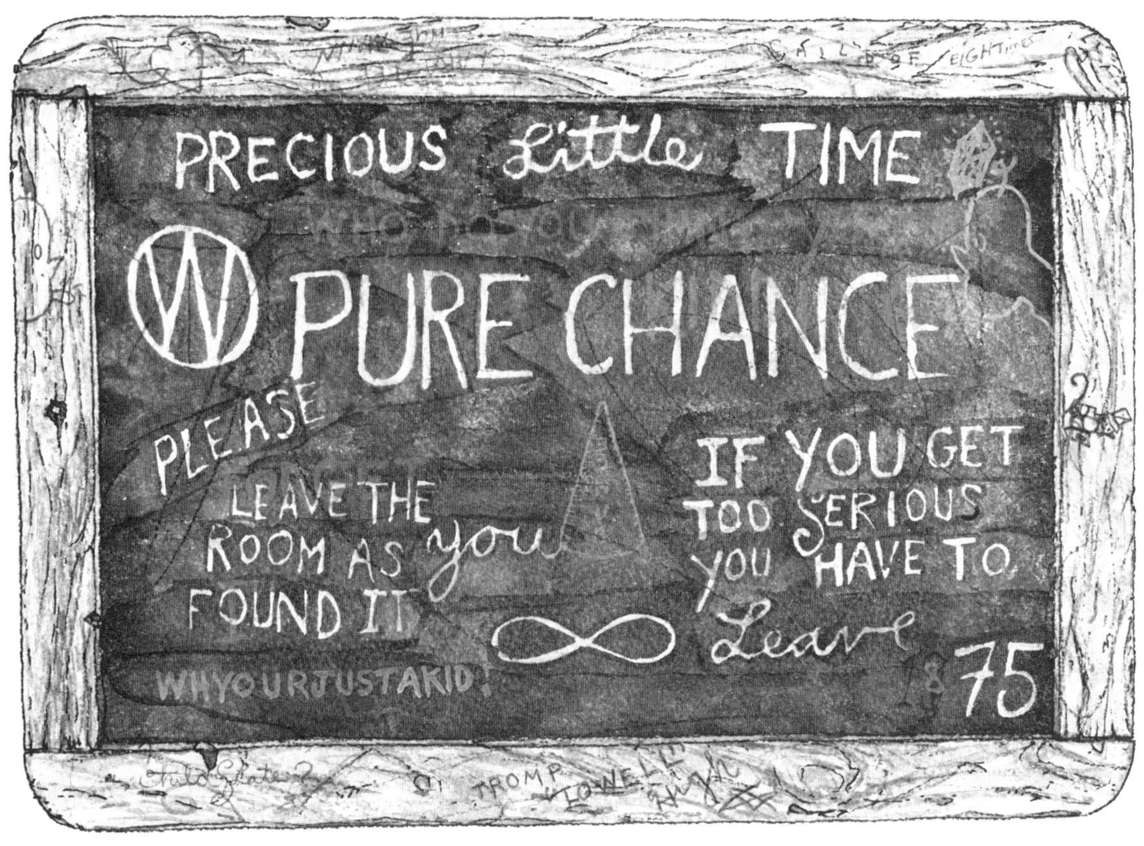

Studease for Post O.O.W. II,
Mr. Unatural Confrontself 1975
watercolor, colored pencil, charcoal and wax
on buff drawing paper
24½ x 36 (irregular)
Collection Louis A. Hermes
San Francisco

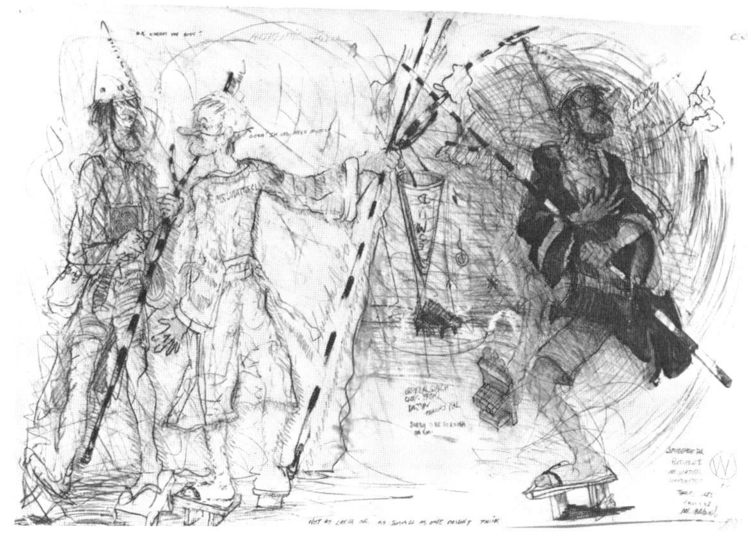

Familiar Forms 1976
charcoal, pastel and wax on buff drawing paper
41½ x 42
Collection Mrs. Julius E. Davis
Minneapolis

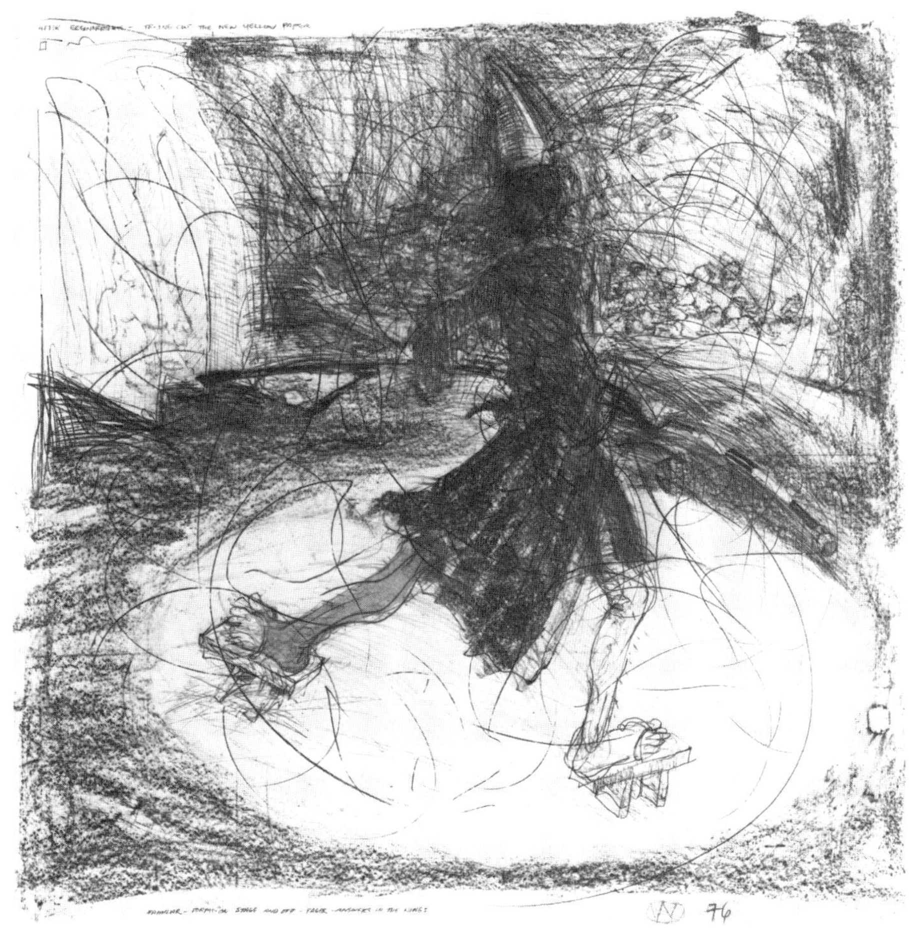

Dr. Hotub 1977
charcoal, colored pencil, watercolor and
wax on parchment
25 x 36
Collection Roxanne Everett-Donald Lippincott
New York

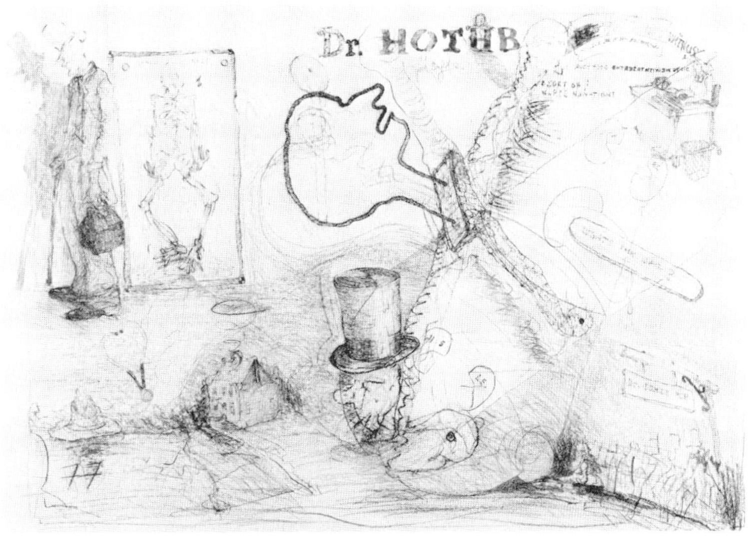

Hound Harbor Forecast 1977
watercolor and ink on paper
22 x 30
Collection Graham Gund
Cambridge, Massachusetts

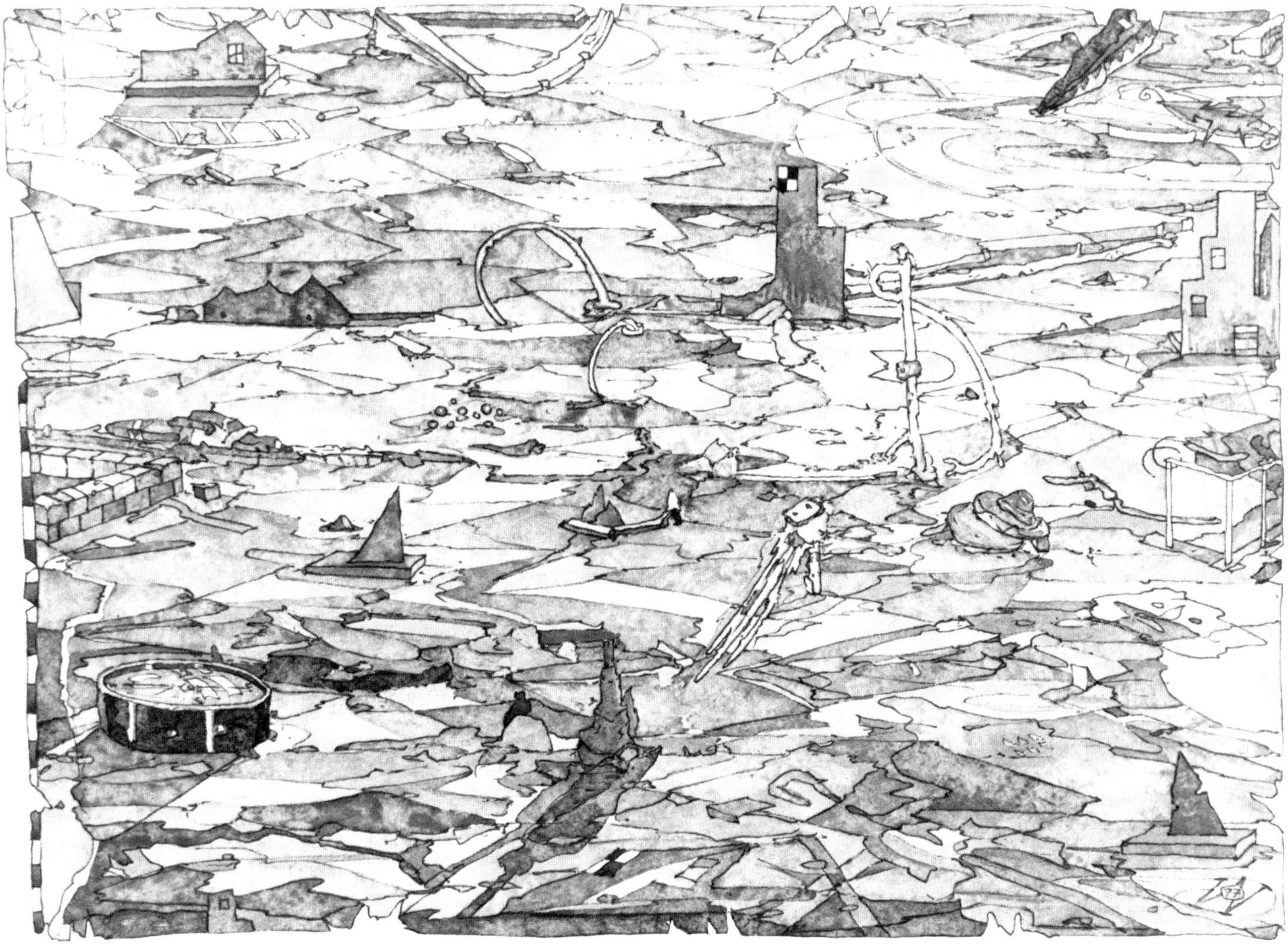

Dutch Interior 1977
colored pencil, charcoal, conte crayon and wax on parchment
25 x 36
Collection Mrs. Alexander de Bretteville
San Francisco

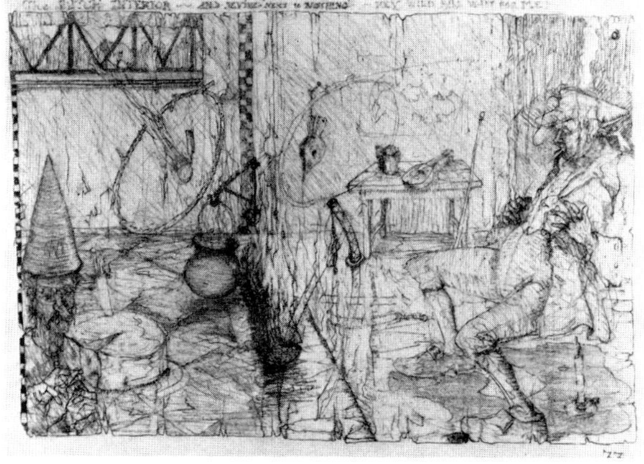

Free's a Bird 1977
colored pencil, charcoal and wax on paper
25 x 36
Courtesy Modesto Lanzone's Restaurant
San Francisco

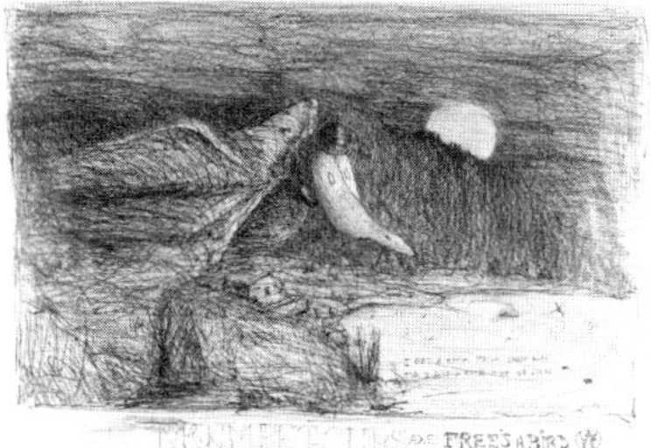

Lil Play on Words 1977
charcoal, conte crayon, ink and graphite
on buff drawing paper
30 x 37½
Collection Mr. and Mrs. William Roth
San Francisco

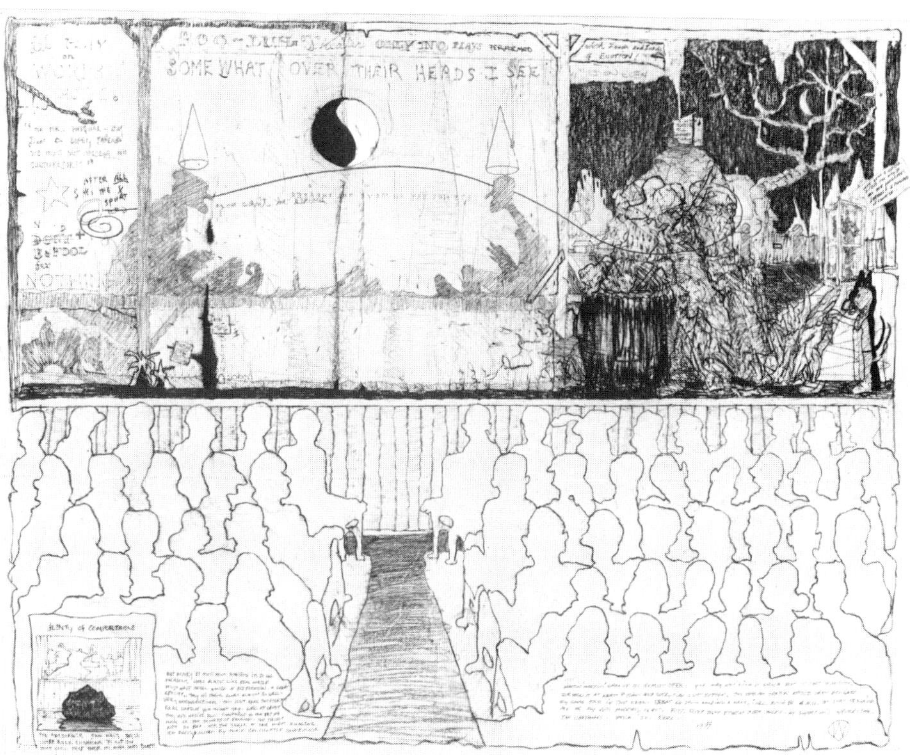

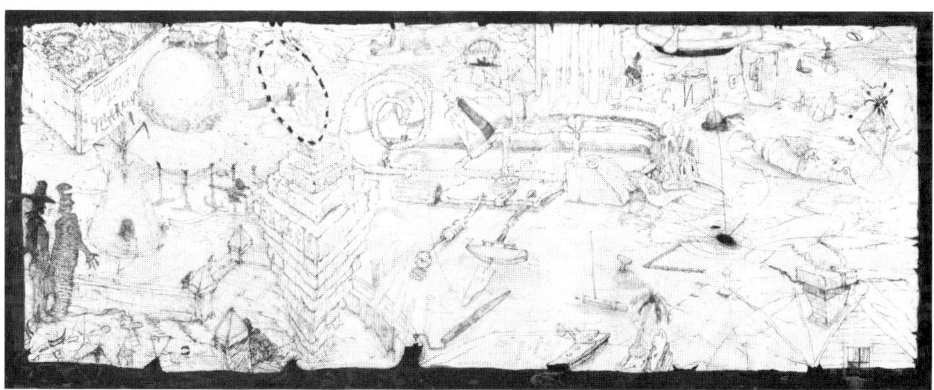

Point Nowhere 1977
charcoal, colored pencil, watercolor and wax
on buff drawing paper
30½ x 75
Private Collection

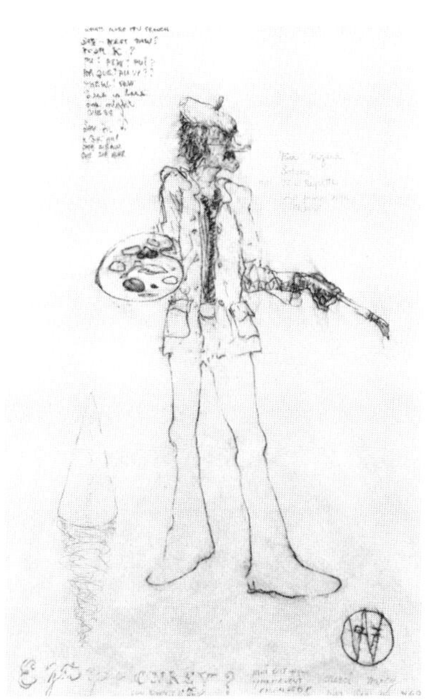

What's More in French 1977
charcoal, colored pencil, wax and ink
on parchment
36 x 25
Private Collection

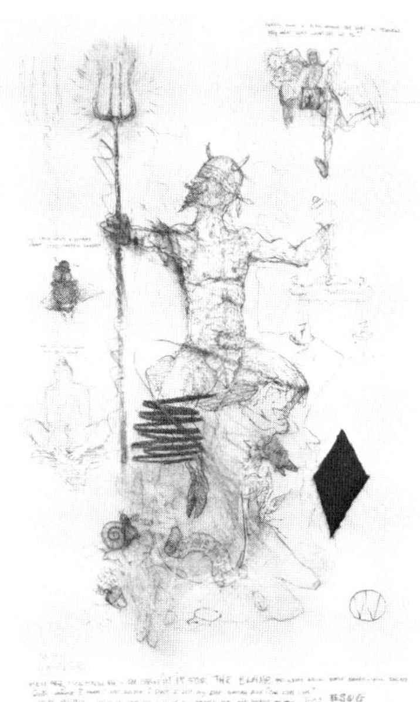

Real Orange Juice 1977
conte crayon, charcoal, colored pencil and wax
on parchment
36 x 24
Collection Robert Arneson and
Sandra Shannonhouse
Benicia, California

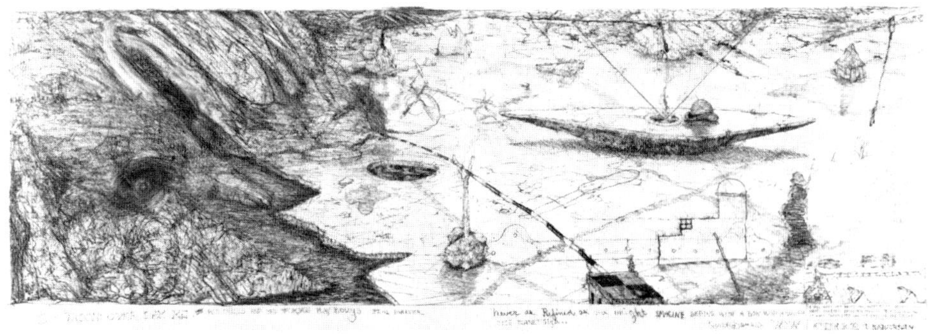

Q.A. Eyes Fishing 1977
charcoal and ink on paper
25 x 72
Collection Yale University Art Gallery
New Haven, Connecticut
Solomon Byron Smith, B.A. 1928, Fund

Eyes Fishing 1977
charcoal and crayon on parchment
25 x 38
Collection Myra and Jim Morgan
Prairie Village, Kansas

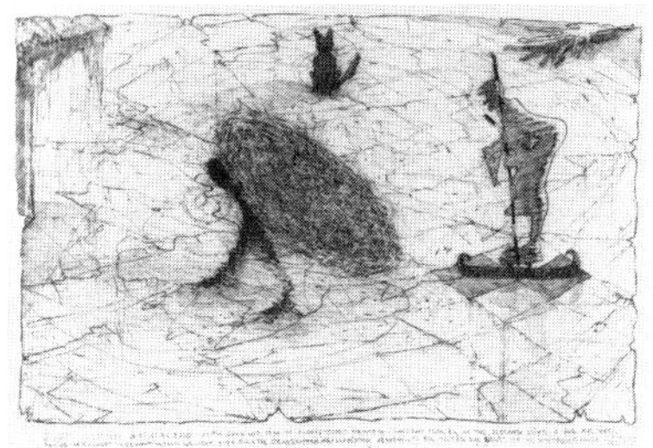

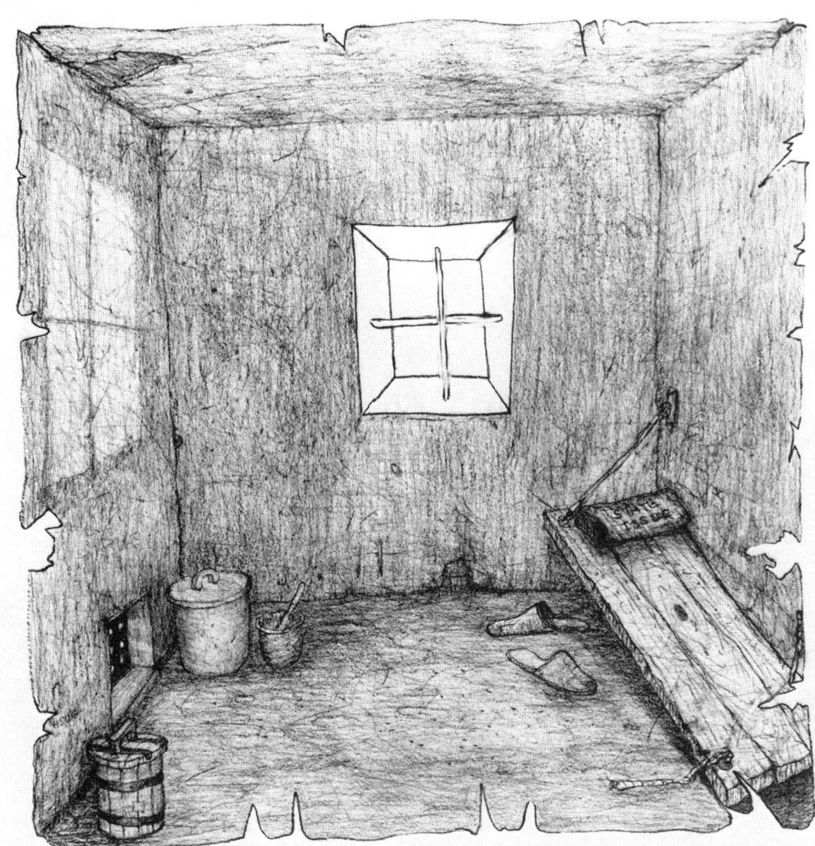

The Prisoner Concept 1977
graphite and wax on parchment
38 x 25⅛
Courtesy Morgan Gallery, Kansas City

Toys of the St. Urchin 1978
watercolor and ink on paper
22 x 30
Collection Indiana University Art Museum
Bloomington

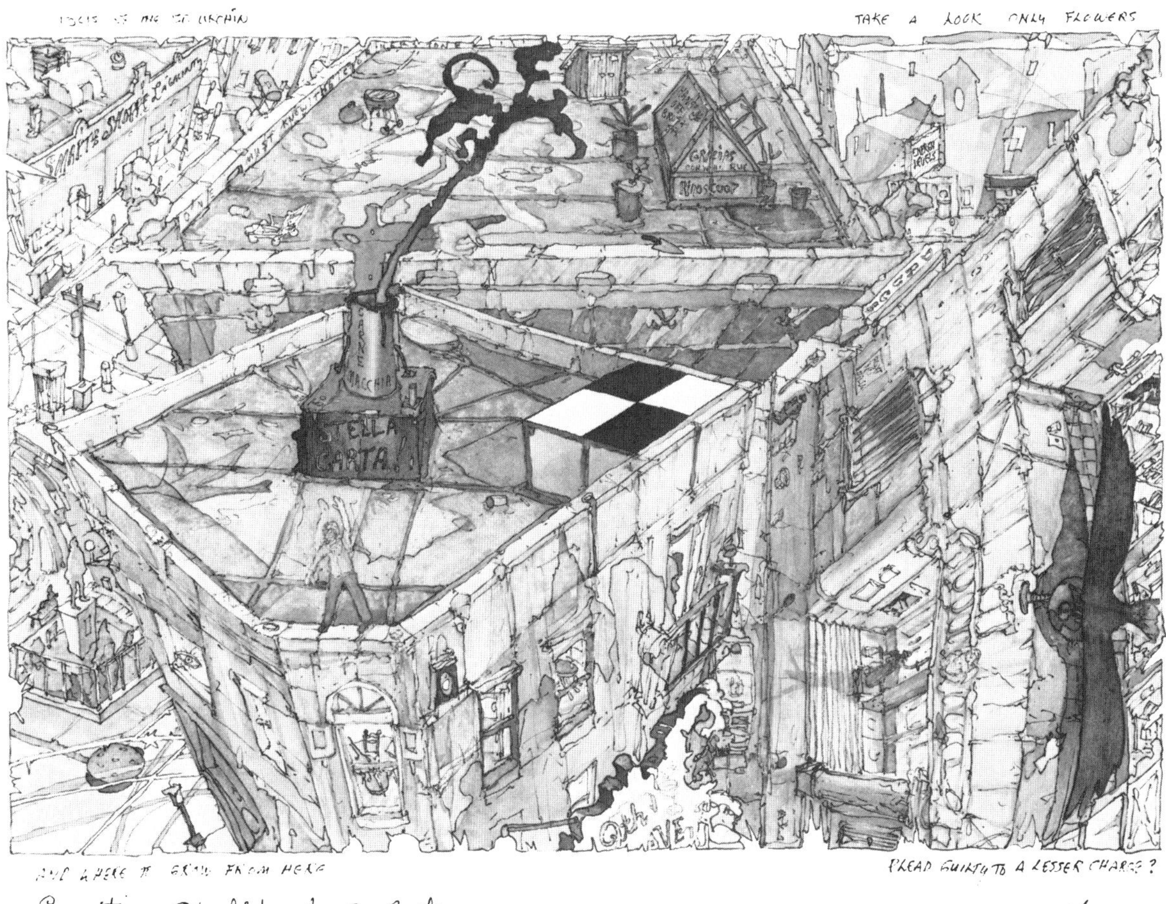

Blue Stump 1978
watercolor and ink on paper
14⅛ x 20
Collection Alice Adam
Chicago

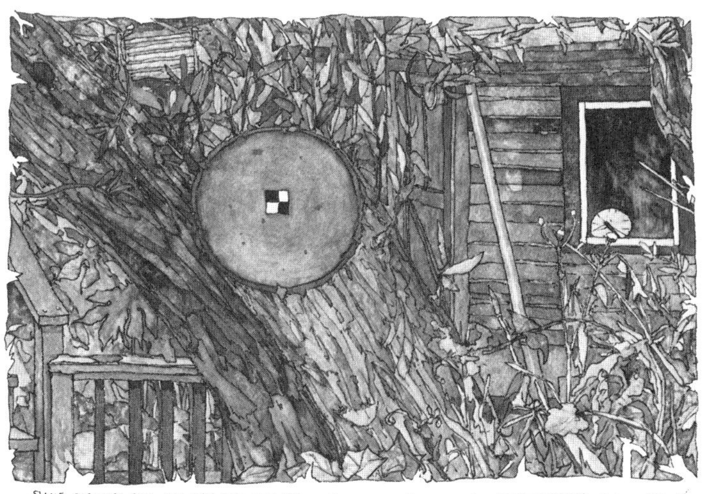

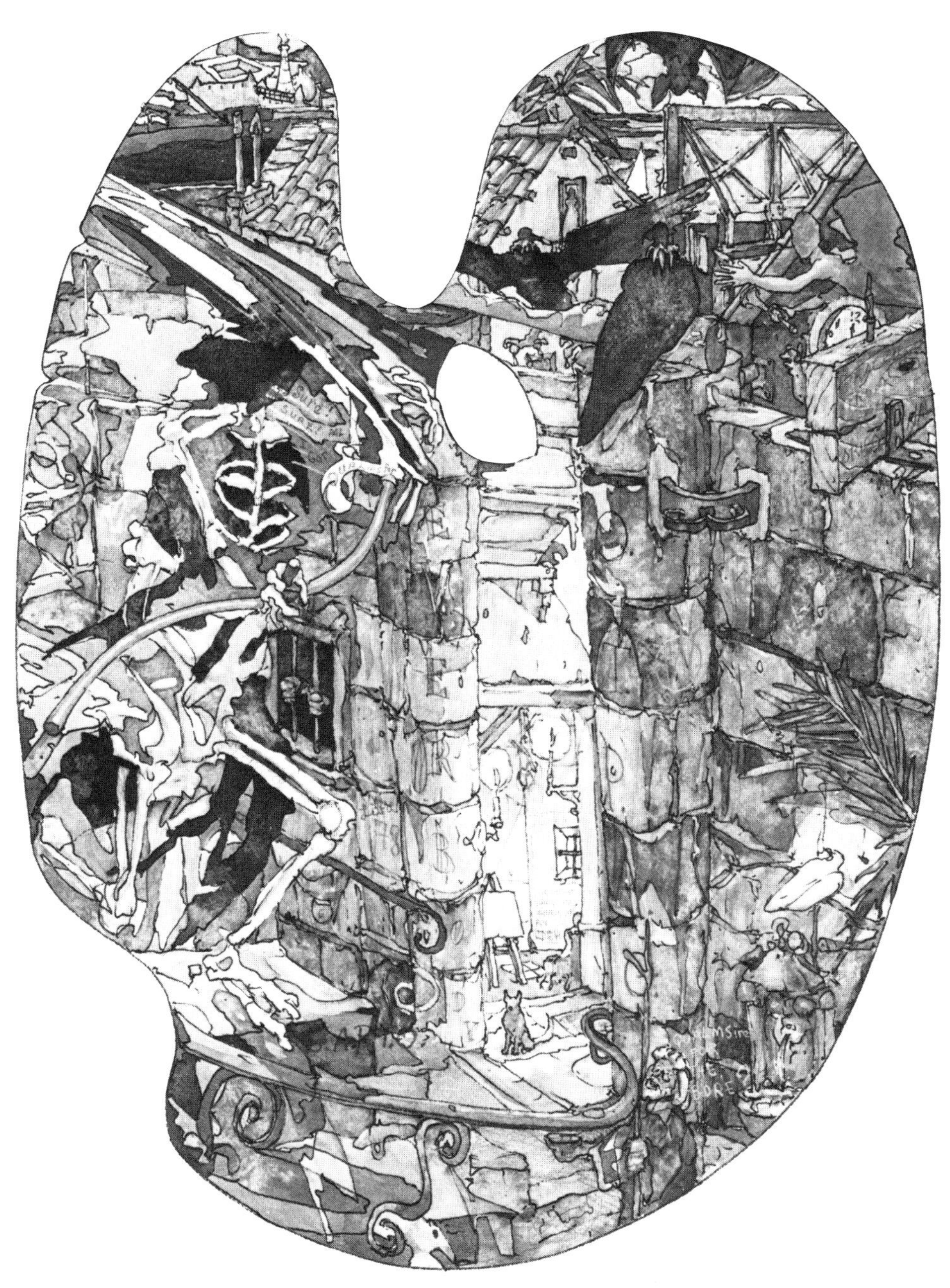

Qualms for the Bore 1978
watercolor, crayon, ink and graphite on paper
30 x 22
Collection the Artist

Constructions

Modern Skullpture with Freaknest 1972
construction of sticks, wood, leather, wire, plastic, glass and found objects
23½ x 127 x 37
Collection Mr. and Mrs. C. David Robinson
Sausalito, California

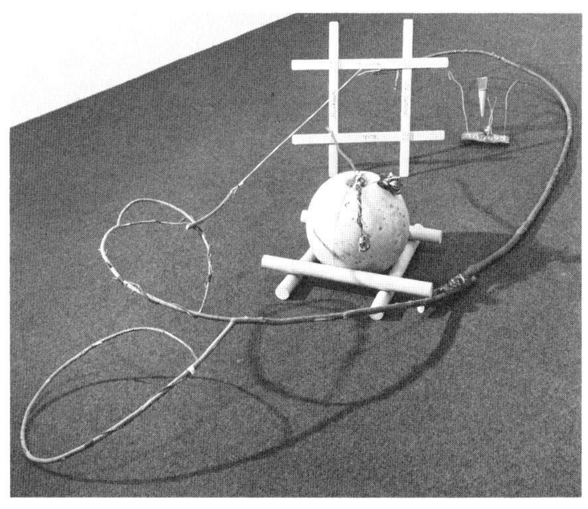

Prisoner Concept 1971
construction of glass, metal, plastic, leather, wood, shovel, fork stick and wooden box filled with felt, ink on chamois hide and found objects
30¼ x 36 x 17
drawing of graphite on paper
18 x 15
Collection David Lawrence
Chicago

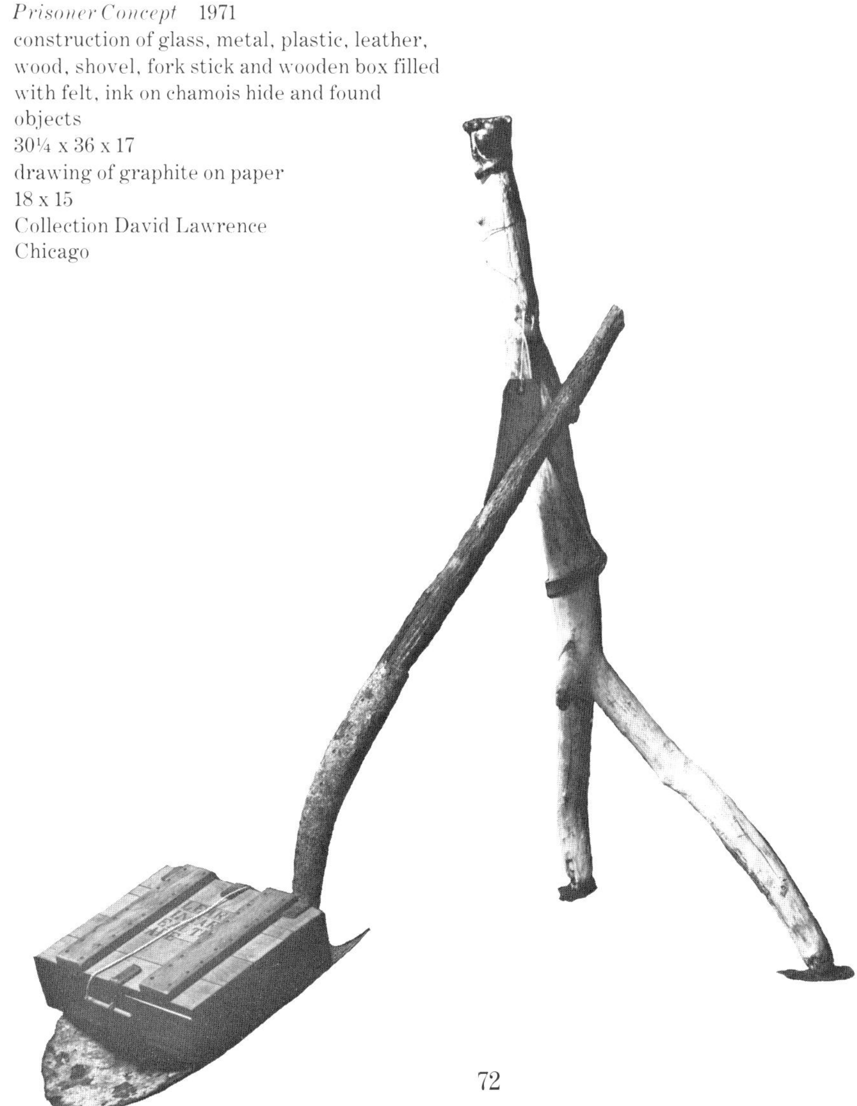

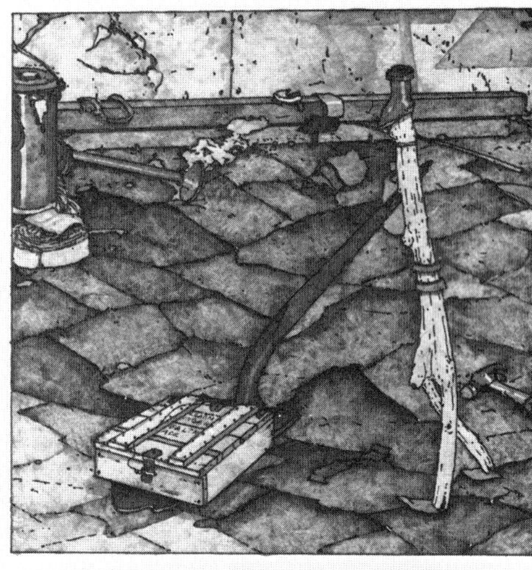

The prisoner Concept
Of who we are and change—as hard to come by as out on the streets. Like the hack saw blade in the cake something to while away the hours and consume—like time what can be said! from the outside—of what? Maybe the concept like the configuration of cell is there to vex your patience blocking moves and energy to discover new paths for itself since it doesn't care what *you* want. It seems to roll away—only like guards and gates when the concept of freedom is a vehicle only—and not necessarily a place to be—and it can leave you wondering what to do with it.

Wm. T. Wiley
1971

Bumpkin 1973
ink on wood, acrylic and ink and lithography on chamois hide, wax, quartz and crystal and metal
20½ x 16
Collection Mr. and Mrs. E. A. Bergman
Chicago

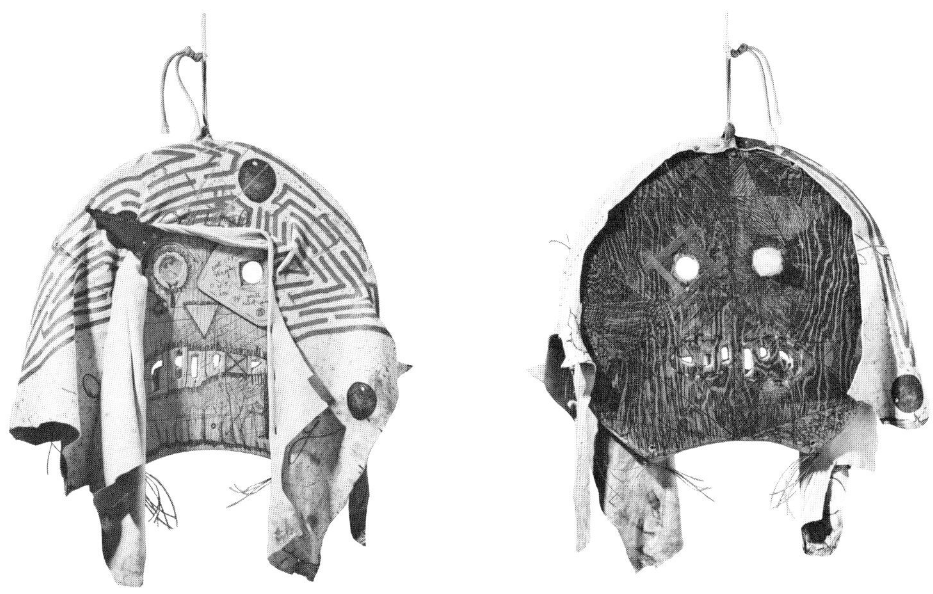

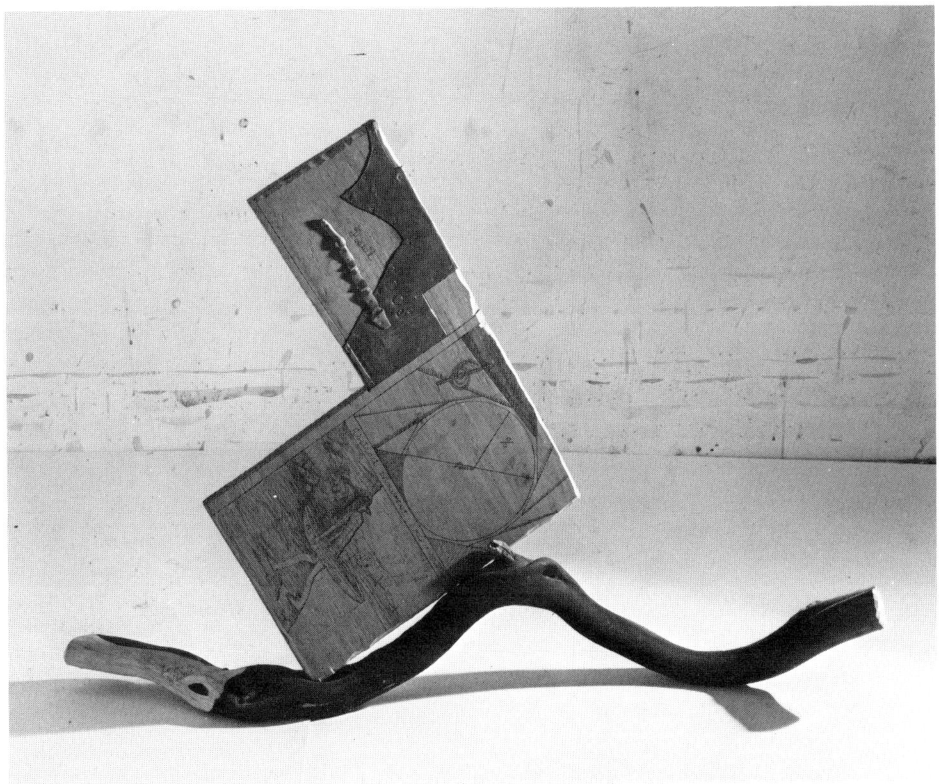

Abstract Involvement 1974
ink and wax on wood, mazanita, lead, metal and bone
21¾ x 31½ x 8
Courtesy Hansen Fuller Goldeen Gallery
San Francisco

B.L.O.T. 1977
watercolor, ink, wax and graphite on wood, wire and cardboard
7 x 14 x 11¼
Courtesy Hansen Fuller Goldeen Gallery
San Francisco

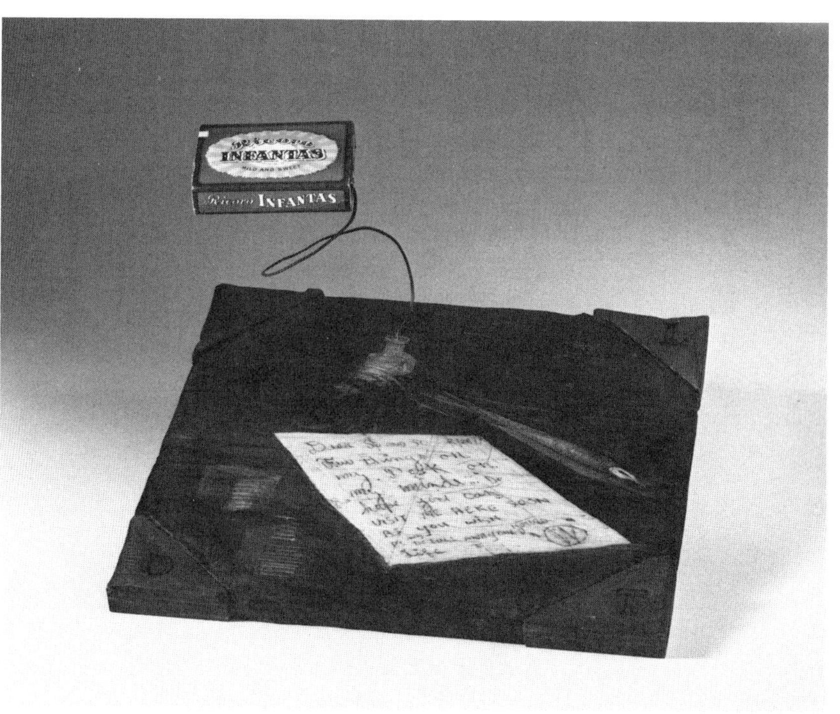

Gospel Tabernacle 1975-77
construction of wood, paint, metal, wire, leather, plastic, lead and ink
36 x 62 x 14
two drawings of graphite and colored pencil on parchment
36 x 25; 25½ x 36
Courtesy Hansen Fuller Goldeen Gallery
San Francisco

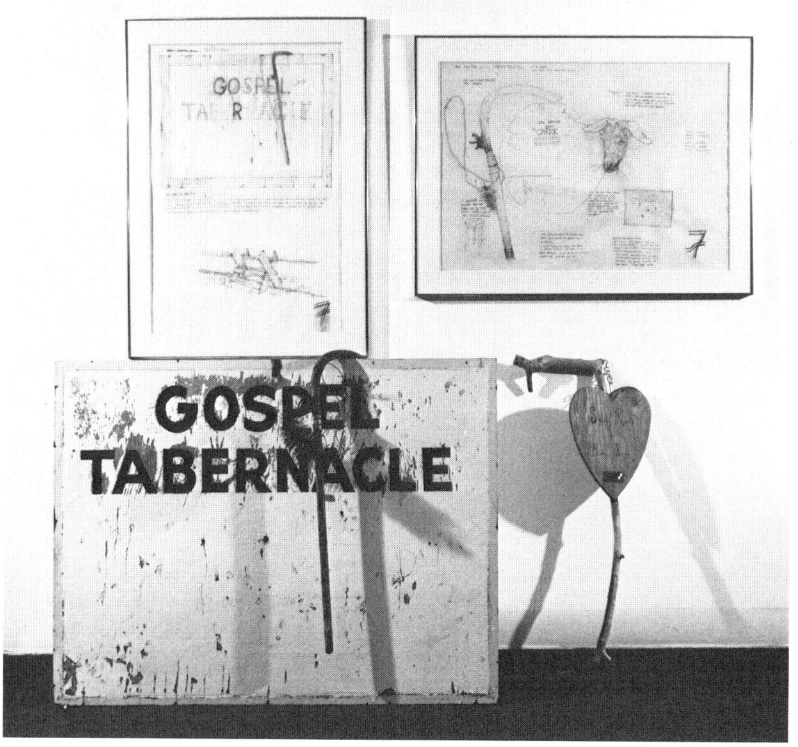

Prints

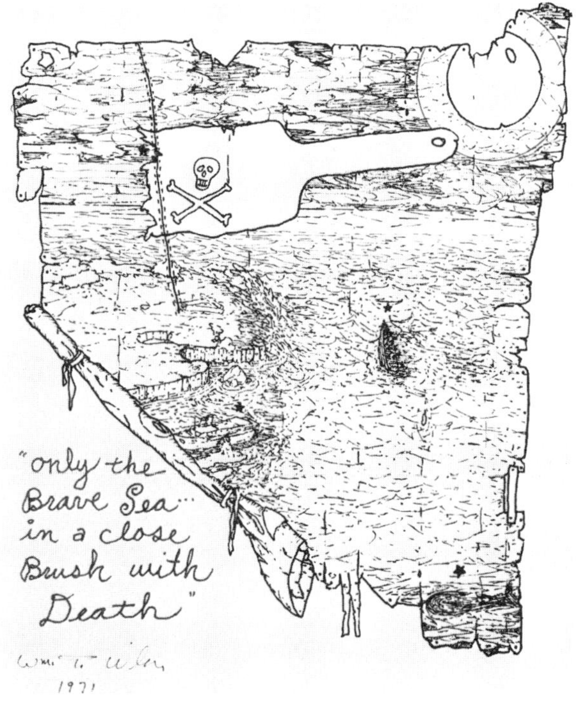

Only the Brave Sea 1971-73
hand-colored offset lithograph on paper
24 x 18
Collection Diana Fuller
San Francisco

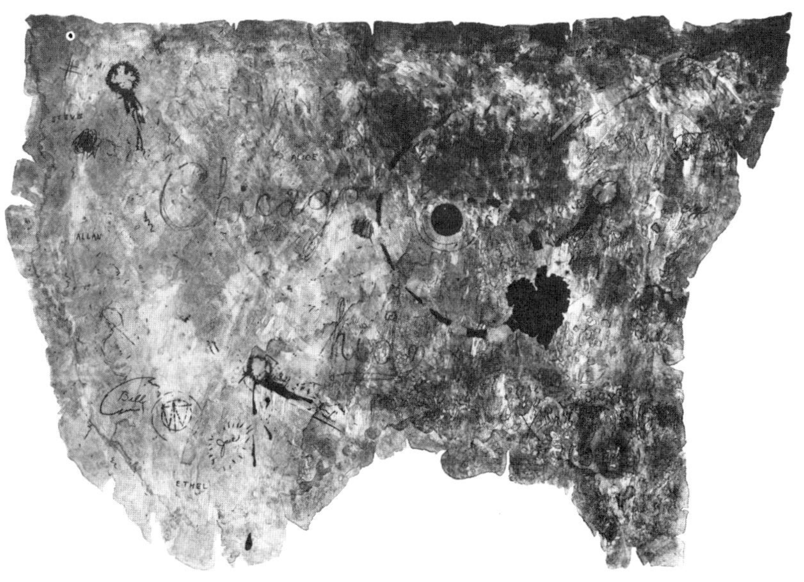

Thank You Hide 1972
five-color lithograph on paper
35 x 48
Courtesy Landfall Press, Inc.
Chicago

The Glittering Remains 1975
etching on paper
20 x 16
Courtesy Landfall Press, Inc.
Chicago

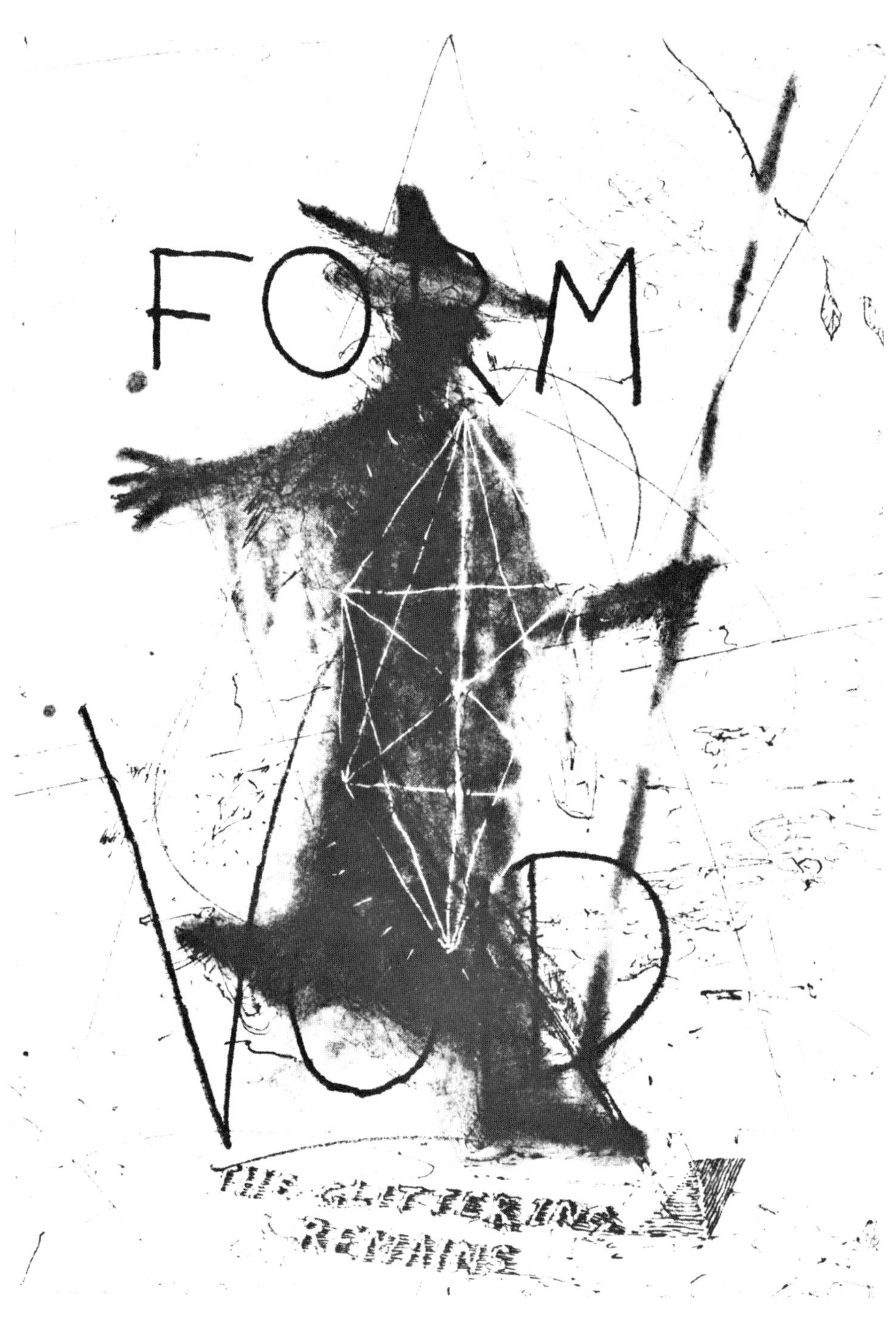

Bullsigh Sea Doubt 1971-73
hand-colored offset lithograph on paper
22¼ x 18¼
Collection Matthew and Wanda Ashe
Sausalito, California

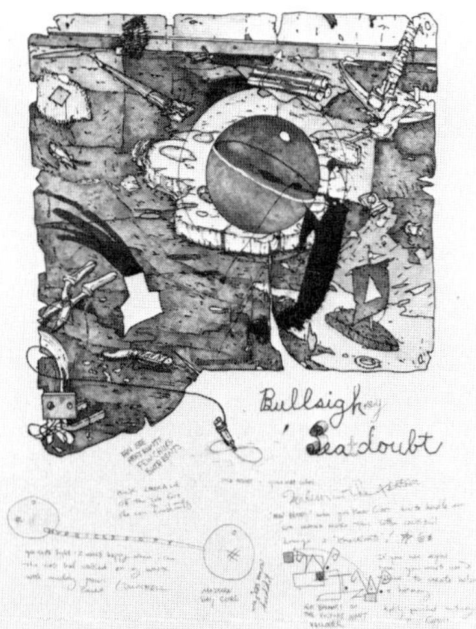

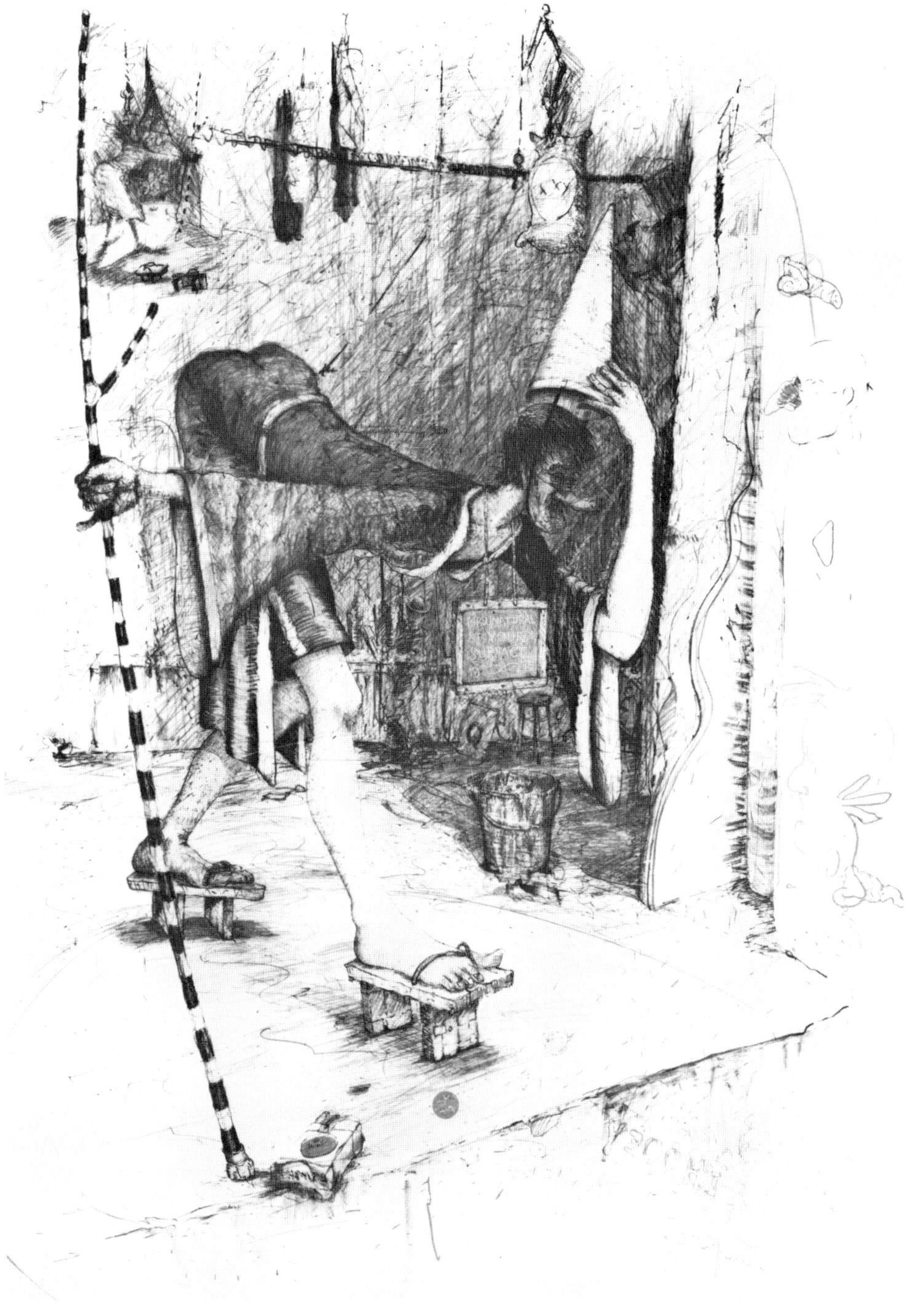

Mr. Unatural 1976
four-color lithograph on paper
36 x 25
Courtesy Landfall Press, Inc.
Chicago

Chronology

1937
Born, Bedford, Indiana, 21 October

1956
Graduates from Columbia High School, Richland, Washington

1959
Marries Dorothy Dowis

1960
B.F.A. degree from the San Francisco Art Institute
A son, Ethan Jacob, is born
Has first one-artist exhibition at the San Francisco Museum of Modern Art

1960-64
Exhibits at the Staempfli Gallery, New York City

1962
M.F.A. degree from the San Francisco Art Institute

1962-73
Teaches at the University of California at Davis

1963
Teaches in the summer session at the San Francisco Art Institute

1965
A son, Zane James, is born

1966
Included in *The Whitney Annual*, Whitney Museum of American Art, New York City

1967
Guest instructor at the University of California, Berkeley; San Francisco Art Institute; University of Nevada, Reno; and Washington State University, Pullman
Completes the film, *The Great Blondino*, with Robert Nelson
Group exhibition, *Funk*, at the University Art Museum, University of California, Berkeley

1968
Guest instructor at the School of Visual Arts, New York City
Visiting artist at the University of Colorado, Boulder
Collaborates with composer, Steve Reich, on the theater event, *Over Evident Falls*
Group exhibition, *Beyond Literalism*, at the Moore College of Art, Philadelphia

1968-79
Exhibits at Hansen Fuller Gallery, San Francisco and Allan Frumkin Gallery, Chicago and New York City

1970
Completes the film, *Man's Nature*

1971-72
One-artist exhibition, *William T. Wiley*, organized by the University Art Museum, University of California, Berkeley, travels to the Institute of Contemporary Art, the University of Pennsylvania, Philadelphia, and the Art Institute of Chicago

1972
Exhibits at *Documenta V*, Kassel, West Germany and the *Venice Biennale*, Venice, Italy

1973
One-artist exhibition, *William T. Wiley*, Stedelijk van Abbemuseum, Eindhoven, The Netherlands

1976
One-artist exhibition in the *Projects* series, The Museum of Modern Art, New York City

1979
Retrospective exhibition, *Wiley Territory*, organized by Walker Art Center, travels to the Dallas Museum of Fine Arts, The Denver Art Museum, the Des Moines Art Center, the San Francisco Museum of Modern Art

Bibliography

Statements by the Artist

"Hides Log—How to Chart a Course." "Sub-Standard Test," "Thoughts On Marcel Duchamp" in *William T. Wiley*. Berkeley: University Art Museum, 1971.

"The Sayings of Lout Sue," published privately with Holbrook Teter, San Francisco, undated (as Wizdumb Gate Press, Brahmagutra, Narayanganj).

Articles and Catalogue Essays

Ashton, Dore. "Abstract Expressionism Isn't Dead," *Studio International*, September 1962, pp 104-105.

__________. "Beyond Literalism, But Not Beyond the Pale," *Arts*, November 1968, p 50.

__________. "Quid est? '. . . for an Answer, only Enigma,'" *Arts*, March 1968, p 48.

Baker, Elizabeth and Raffaele, Joseph. "Way Out West: Interviews With 4 San Francisco Artists," *Art News*, Summer 1967, pp 38-40.

Coffelt, Beth. "Beyond the Flesh, Beyond the Bone," *San Francisco Sunday Examiner & Chronicle*, May 29, 1977, pp 20-24.

Dunham, Judith L. "William Wiley Travels Life," *Artweek*, January 21, 1978, pp 1, 16.

Frankenstein, Alfred. "The Special Insight of William T. Wiley," *San Francisco Sunday Examiner & Chronicle*, September 26, 1971, pp 41-42.

Glueck, Grace. "The Slant Step," *The New York Times*, June 2, 1968, Section 2, p 22.

Hughes, Robert. "Quirky Angler," *Time*, January 17, 1972, p 38.

Hull, Roger. "Frisco's William Wiley Teases Viewer with Varied Visual Puns," *The Sunday Oregonian*, Portland, December 14, 1975, p 19.

Kenedy, R. C. "Paris," *Art International*, July-August 1977, p 61.

Kramer, Hilton. "Wiley of the West: Dude Ranch Dada," *The New York Times*, May 16, 1971, p 19.

Leering, J. "William T. Wiley." *Eindhoven: Van Abbemuseum*, 1973.

McCann, Cecile N. "Probing the Western Ethic," *Artweek*, May 15, 1971.

Mellow, James R. "Realist William Wiley," *The New York Times*, October 11, 1970, Section 2, p 23.

"The New/New Criticism," *Time*, May 31, 1968, pp 46-49.

Perreault, John. "Beyond Literalism," *Art International*, January 1969, p 37+.

__________. "Eccentrics," *The Village Voice*, October 15, 1970, pp 18, 20.

__________. "Metaphysical Funk Monk," *Art News*, May 1968, pp 52-53+.

__________. "Towards a New Metaphysics," *The Village Voice*, September 1967.

Raymond, Herbert. "Prince of Wizdumb," *Art and Artists*, November 1973, pp 24-27.

Richardson, Brenda. "I am My Own Enigma," in *William T. Wiley*. Berkeley, 1971

Selz, Peter. "Six Artists in Search of a Definition of San Francisco," *Art News*, Summer 1973, pp 34-37.

Tooker, Dan. "How to Chart a Course: An Interview with William T. Wiley," *Artscanada*, Spring 1974, pp 82-85.

Wasserman, Emily. "William T. Wiley and William Allan: Meditations at Fort Prank," *Artforum*, December 1970, pp 62-67.

White, Robin. "Interview with William T. Wiley," *View*, May 1979.

Reviews

Andre, Michael. One-man exhibitions, The Museum of Modern Art, New York; Allan Frumkin Gallery, New York, *Art News*, Summer 1976, pp 173-174.

Ashton, Dore. "New York Commentary," *Studio International*, July 1968, p 37.

Martin, Henry. "From Milan and Turin: William Wiley," *Art International*, December 20, 1971, pp 74-75.

Richardson, Brenda. "I am My Own Enigma," in *William T. Wiley*. Berkeley: University Art Museum 1971.

Trini, Tommaso. "Exhibitions," *Domus*, November 1971, p 53.

Colophon

This catalogue was printed on Mohawk Superfine papers by Colormaster Press. The type is 8, 9 and 10 point Century Expanded set on a V-I-P by Typehouse/Duragraph. Designed by Robert Jensen.

Staff List

Registrar
Gwen Bitz
Graphic Design
Robert Jensen
Catalogue
Mildred S. Friedman
Wayne Henrikson
Linda Krenzin
Mary Unthank
Installation
Terry Fisher
Tom Briggs
Steve Ecklund
Ron Elliott
James Gonsoski
Hugh Jacobson
John King
Paul Rumme
Tim Solien
Arthur Stein
Lee Witcher
Photography
Tom Arndt
Glenn Halvorson
Public Information
Kathe Kertz Stanton
Karen Statler
Research Assistance
Trent Myers,
National Endowment for the Arts Intern

Photo Credits

Tom Arndt and Glenn Halvorson: pp 14, 29, 36, 40, p 42 (top), p 52 (bottom left), p 57 (left), p 58 (top), p 60 (bottom), p 61 (bottom), p 62 (top left), p 65 (top, bottom), p 67 (top right, bottom), p 70 (bottom), p 71, p 72 (bottom), p 75 (bottom), p 76, p 77 (right)
Rudolph Burckhardt, courtesy Leo Castelli Gallery: p 10 (left)
Geoffrey Clements, courtesy Whitney Museum of American Art: p 8; courtesy Odyssia Gallery: p 59
Courtesy Dallas Museum of Fine Arts: p 30 (top)
Courtesy The Denver Art Museum: p 39
eeva-inkeri, courtesy Allan Frumkin Gallery: p 31 (bottom), p 55 (bottom), p 56, p 62 (top right), p 72 (top)
Lee Fatherree: pp 22, 26, p 27 (top), p 30 (bottom), p 48 (bottom), p 52 (top), p 53, p 54 (top, bottom right), p 57 (right), p 58 (bottom), p 66 (bottom), p 67 (top left), p 68 (top left, right), p 74 (bottom), p 75 (top), p 77 (left)
Courtesy The Fort Worth Art Museum: p 50 (top)
Courtesy Allan Frumkin Gallery: p 18, p 27 (bottom), p 44, p 63 (top right), p 69 (top left, right), p 73 (bottom)
Courtesy Hansen Fuller Goldeen Gallery: pp 19, 28, p 42 (bottom), pp 43, 45, p 48 (top left), p 52 (bottom right), p 54 (bottom left), p 66 (top), p 68 (bottom), p 69 (top left, right), p 73 (bottom)
X. de Gery: p 60 (top)
Courtesy Indiana University Art Museum: p 70 (top)
Bruce C. Jones, courtesy Xavier Fourcade, Inc.: p 12
Courtesy Los Angeles County Museum of Art: p 38
Courtesy The Minneapolis Institute of Arts: p 9
Otto E. Nelson, courtesy Allan Frumkin Gallery: p 10 (center)
Nobody Prints/Joe Nobody, courtesy Allan Frumkin Gallery: p 11
Judy Olausen: Wiley portrait
Eric Pollitzer, courtesy Des Moines Art Center: p 16
Professional Litho Art, Inc.: front cover, pp 6, 20, 24, 32, 34, 46, back cover
Courtesy San Francisco Museum of Modern Art: p 37 (top)
Schopplein Studio, courtesy Hansen Fuller Goldeen Gallery: p 23, p 31 (top), p 37 (bottom), p 41, p 48 (top right), p 49 (top, bottom), p 50 (bottom), p 51, p 55 (top), p 61 (top left, right, p 62 (bottom left, right), p 63 (top left), p 64 (top, bottom), p 73 (top), p 74 (top)

Back cover:

What's Left of the Garden and Mirror 1973
watercolor, ink and colored pencil on paper
30 x 22
Collection Mr. and Mrs C. David Robinson
Sausalito, California

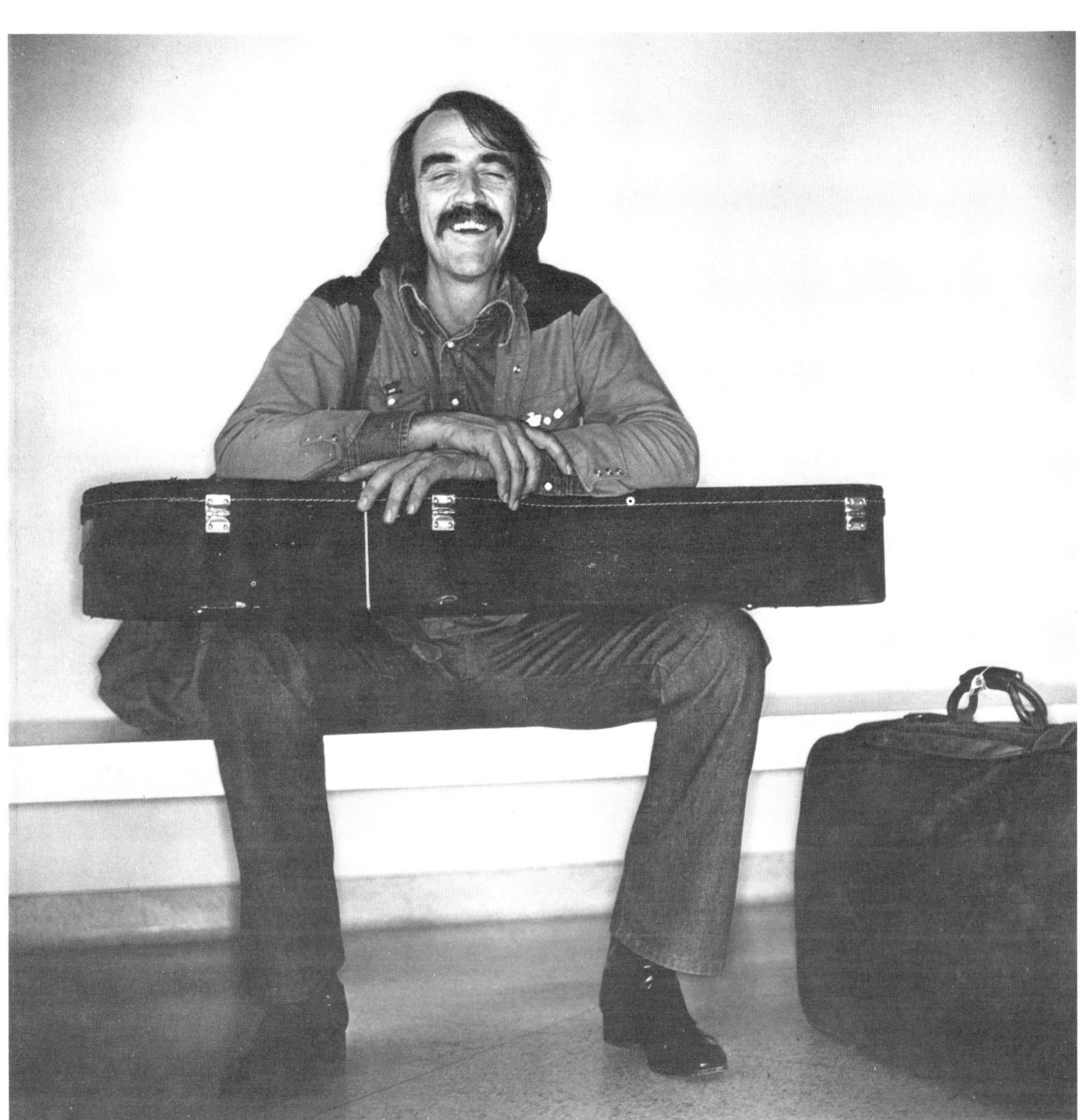

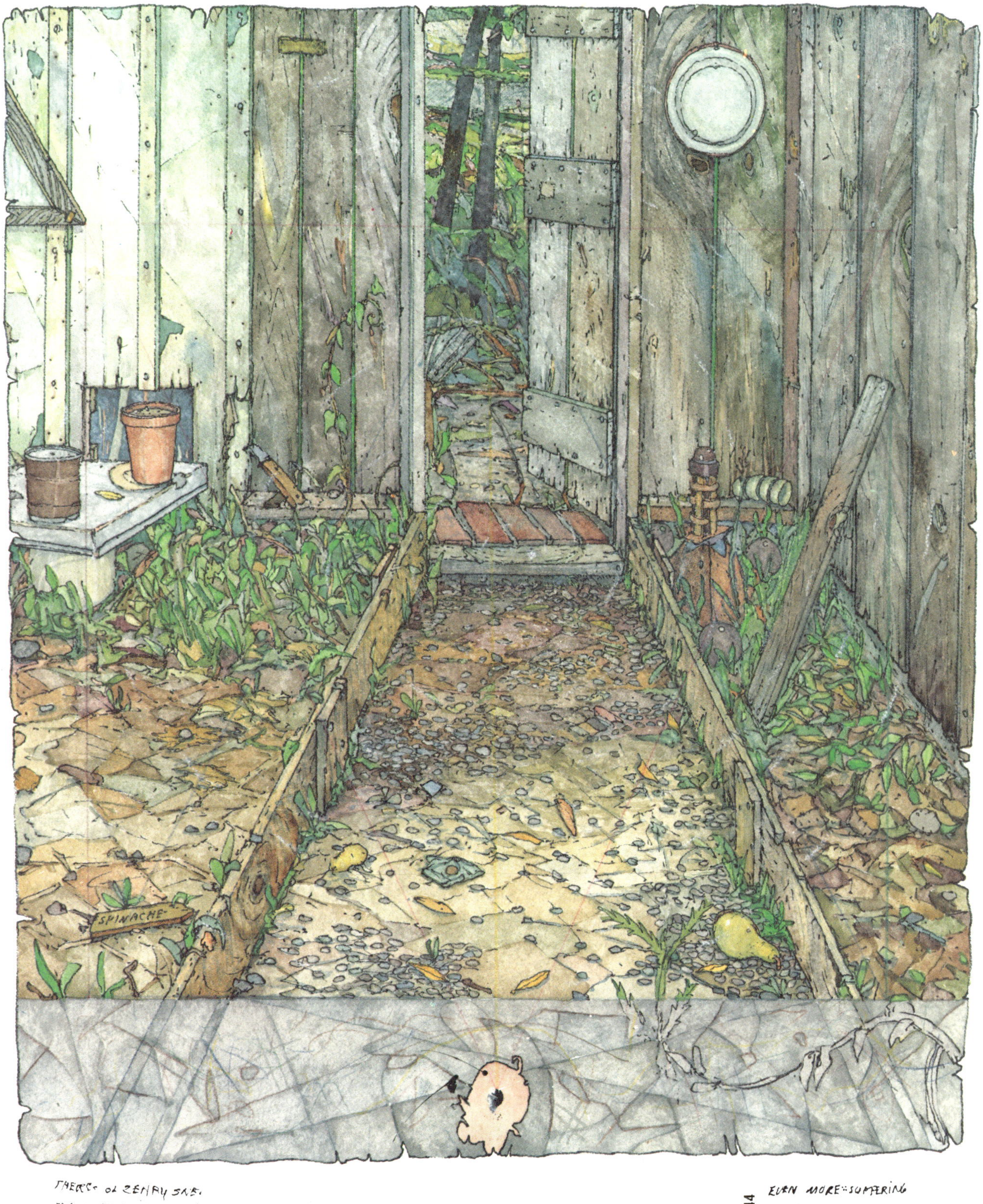

THE USUAL::AFFLICTED:: HANDIC
WHY:: THERES NO MARGIN FO
TO A SMALL PLAT OF A

APEX

TP_CQ

9780935640007

76670941 – 44

EVEN MORE::SUFFERING
ND ONLY A SCREEN TEST::
SCHARACTERS TRAIT
TO PROTECT THE PLAN.